Contents

Chapter 1: News and Statistics

Chapter 2: Impact and Attitudes

Chapter 3: Refugees

Introduction

MIGRATION & IMMIGRATION is Volume 359 in the *ISSUES* series. The aim of the series is to offer current, diverse information about important issues in our world, from a UK perspective.

ABOUT MIGRATION & IMMIGRATION

Migration and immigration is a complex and often controversial topic, particularly in light of Brexit and the ongoing refugee crisis. This book looks at immigrants, asylum seekers and refugees. It considers the push and pull factors behind the different types of migration, our attitudes towards immigration and the contribution migrants make to our society.

OUR SOURCES

Titles in the *ISSUES* series are designed to function as educational resource books, providing a balanced overview of a specific subject.

The information in our books is comprised of facts, articles and opinions from many different sources, including:

◆ Newspaper reports and opinion pieces

◆ Website factsheets

◆ Magazine and journal articles

◆ Statistics and surveys

◆ Government reports

◆ Literature from special interest groups.

A NOTE ON CRITICAL EVALUATION

Because the information reprinted here is from a number of different sources, readers should bear in mind the origin of the text and whether the source is likely to have a particular bias when presenting information (or when conducting their research). It is hoped that, as you read about the many aspects of the issues explored in this book, you will critically evaluate the information presented.

It is important that you decide whether you are being presented with facts or opinions. Does the writer give a biased or unbiased report? If an opinion is being expressed, do you agree with the writer? Is there potential bias to the 'facts' or statistics behind an article?

ASSIGNMENTS

In the back of this book, you will find a selection of assignments designed to help you engage with the articles you have been reading and to explore your own opinions. Some tasks will take longer than others and there is a mixture of design, writing and research-based activities that you can complete alone or in a group.

FURTHER RESEARCH

At the end of each article we have listed its source and a website that you can visit if you would like to conduct your own research. Please remember to critically evaluate any sources that you consult and consider whether the information you are viewing is accurate and unbiased.

Useful Websites

www.capx.co

www.gov.uk

www.independent.co.uk

www.ippr.org

www.migrationobservatory.ox.ac.uk

www.news-decoder.com

www.ons.gov.uk

www.redcross.org.uk

www.refugee-action.org

www.refugeecouncil.org.uk

www.telegraph.co.uk

www.theconversation.com

www.theguardian.com

www.theweek.co.uk

www.unhcr.org

www.weforum.org

www.yougov.co.uk

Summary of latest statistics

Latest figures from the Home Office

1. How many people come to the UK each year (including visitors)?

There were an estimated 144.7 million passenger arrivals in the year ending June 2019 (including returning UK residents), a 4% increase compared to the previous year and the highest number on record. The latest available data (relating to year ending March 2019) show arrivals from British, other European Economic Area (EEA) and Swiss nationals increased by 7% to 124.4 million, while arrivals from Non-EEA nationals decreased by 7% to 19.6 million.

There were 3.0 million visas granted in the year ending June 2019, a 9% increase of 249,279 compared with the previous year, continuing the upward trend seen over the last decade. Of these, over three-quarters (77%) were to visit, 8% were to study (excluding short-term study), 6% were to work and 2% were for family reasons.

2. Why do people come to the UK?

2.1 Work

There were 185,465 work-related visas granted in the year ending June 2019, 11% higher than the previous year, and the highest level since the year ending March 2009.

The majority (69%) of the increase in the latest year can be accounted for by Skilled (Tier 2) work visas, which increased by 13% to 108,890 following a relatively stable period between 2015 and 2018. This category accounts for 59% of work-related visas granted.

There were also increase in the number of Youth mobility and temporary worker (Tier 5) visas granted, up 7% to 43,122, and an increase in High-value (Tier 1) visas granted (up 36% to 7,492).

2.2 Study

In the year ending June 2019, there were 253,111 Sponsored study (Tier 4) visas granted (including dependants), a 13% increase or 29,115 more than the previous year, and the highest level since 2011.

The majority (85%) of those applying to come to the UK on a sponsored study visa apply to study at Higher Education (university) institutions. In the year ending June 2019, Sponsored study visa applications for the Higher Education (university) sector increased by 11% to 201,919, the highest level on record.

2.3 Family

There were 169,606 visas granted for family reasons in the year ending June 2019, 20% more than in the previous year.

There was a large increase in EEA family permits granted, up 53% to 44,825, as well as increases in family-related visas granted (up 16% to 49,741) and dependants of people coming to the UK on other types of visas (up 9% to 74,518).

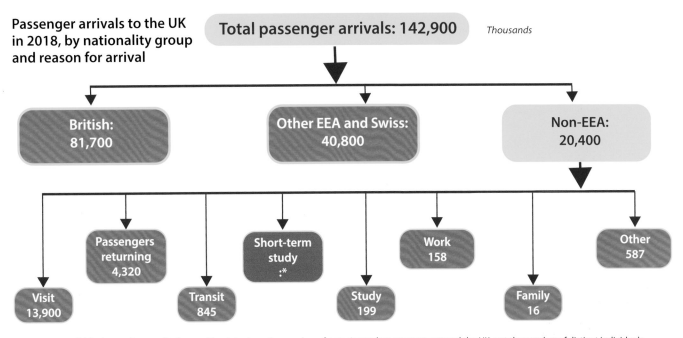

Passenger arrivals to the UK in 2018, by nationality group and reason for arrival

Total passenger arrivals: 142,900 *Thousands*

- British: 81,700
- Other EEA and Swiss: 40,800
- Non-EEA: 20,400
  - Passengers returning 4,320
  - Visit 13,900
  - Transit 845
  - Short-term study :*
  - Study 199
  - Work 158
  - Family 16
  - Other 587

*Data not available due to data quality issues. The data show the number of occasions when a person entered the UK, not the number of distinct individuals.
Data on reason for arrival for British, EEA and Swiss nationals are not collected.

3. How many people do we grant asylum or protection to?

The UK gave protection to 18,519 people in the year ending June 2019 (up 29% compared with the previous year). This was the highest number of people granted protection in the UK over a one-year period since the year ending September 2003.

Since it began in 2014, 17,051 people have been resettled under the Vulnerable Person Resettlement Scheme (VPRS), with 4,200 being resettled in the year ending June 2019.

There were 32,693 asylum applications in the UK in the year ending June 2019, 21% more than the previous year but below the level seen in the year ending June 2016 during the European migration crisis.

In the year ending June 2019, 44% of initial decisions on asylum applications resulted in a grant, compared with 29% in the previous year. However, the grant rate at final decision (following appeal) increased to around 50% (based on data from 2015 to 2017).

3.1 Asylum claims on the basis of sexual orientation (experimental statistics)

In 2018, there were 1,502 asylum applications where sexual orientation formed part of the basis for the claim (LGB asylum applications), representing 5% of all applications.

Although the grant rate for LGB asylum applications was lower than for all asylum applications (35%), nationalities who commonly claim asylum on the basis of sexual orientation typically see higher grant rates for LGB applications than for total applications.

4. How many people continue their stay in the UK?

4.1 Extension of temporary stay in the UK

There were 267,951 grants of extension of stay in the year ending June 2019, an increase of 14% on the previous year.

The number of extensions for work reasons increased by 20% to 95,507 including increases in the Skilled (Tier 2) work category. There was also a 16% increase in extensions for family reasons to 104,644.

4.2 Settlement

There were 89,406 decisions on applications for settlement in the UK in the year ending June 2019, 4% more than in the previous year. Of these, 85,931 (96%) resulted in a grant. This was an increase for the second consecutive year, following falls since the year ending June 2013.

4.3 Citizenship

There were 175,011 applications for British citizenship in the year to June 2019, 19% more than in the previous year. Applications for citizenship by EU nationals increased by 26% to 53,588. Increases in citizenship applications from EU nationals in the last three years are likely to result from more people seeking to confirm their status following the EU referendum.

Applications made by non-EU nationals increased by 17% in the most recent year to 121,423, following falls in the previous two years.

5. How many people are detained or returned?

5.1 Immigration detention

At the end of June 2019, there were 1,727 people held in the detention estate, 22% fewer than a year earlier.

In the year ending June 2019, 24,052 individuals entered the detention estate, 8% fewer than the previous year. This represents a fall for the fourth consecutive year to the lowest level since comparable records began in 2009.

In 2018, one person died while being held solely under immigration powers in detention. This does not include those who died while being detained solely under immigration powers in prison, or after leaving detention.

5.2 Returns

There were 8,060 enforced returns from the UK in the year ending June 2019, 26% fewer than the previous year (10,914). This was largely accounted for by falls in enforced returns of people who were in detention prior to their return, which fell by 25% to 5,395.

Additionally, there were 13,140 voluntary returns (although this figure is subject to upward revision), and 19,399 passengers refused entry at port and subsequently departed.

22 August 2019

Which countries have the most immigrants?

This article is published in collaboration with **The Conversation.**

By Gilles Pison, Professor at the National Museum of Natural History and Associate Researcher at INED, National Museum of Natural History (MNHN) - Sorbonne Universités

The proportion of immigrants varies considerably from one country to another. In some, it exceeds half the population, while in others it is below 0.1%. Which countries have the most immigrants? Where do they come from? How are they distributed across the world? We provide here an overview of the number and share of immigrants in different countries around the world.

According to the United Nations, the United States has the highest number of immigrants (foreign-born individuals), with 48 million in 2015, five times more than in Saudi Arabia (11 million) and six times more than in Canada (7.6 million) (figure below). However, in proportion to their population size, these two countries have significantly more immigrants: 34% and 21%, respectively, versus 15% in the United States.

Looking at the ratio of immigrants to the total population), countries with a high proportion of immigrants can be divided into five groups:

- The first group comprises countries that are sparsely populated but have abundant oil resources, where immigrants sometimes outnumber the native-born population. In 2015, the world's highest proportions of immigrants were found in this group: United Arab Emirates (87%), Kuwait (73%), Qatar (68%), Saudi Arabia, Bahrain and Oman, where the proportion ranges from 34% to 51%.

- The second group consists of very small territories, microstates, often with special tax rules: Macao (57%), Monaco (55%) and Singapore (46%).

The 15 countries with the most immigrants (in millions)

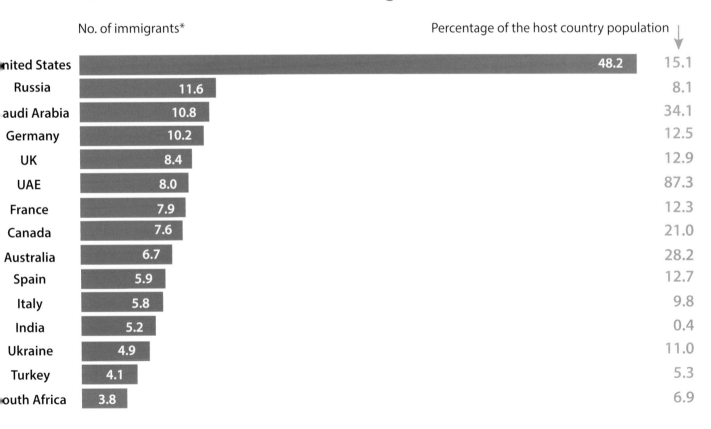

No. of immigrants*

Percentage of the host country population

Country	No. of immigrants*	Percentage of the host country population
United States	48.2	15.1
Russia	11.6	8.1
Saudi Arabia	10.8	34.1
Germany	10.2	12.5
UK	8.4	12.9
UAE	8.0	87.3
France	7.9	12.3
Canada	7.6	21.0
Australia	6.7	28.2
Spain	5.9	12.7
Italy	5.8	9.8
India	5.2	0.4
Ukraine	4.9	11.0
Turkey	4.1	5.3
South Africa	3.8	6.9

*Foreign born

G.Pison, *Population & Societies* no 563, 2019.

- The third group is made up of nations formerly designated as 'new countries', which cover vast territories but are still sparsely populated: Australia (28%) and Canada (21%).

- The fourth group, which is similar to the third in terms of mode of development, is that of Western industrial democracies, in which the proportion of immigrants generally ranges from 9% to 17%: Austria (17%), Sweden (16%), United States (15%), United Kingdom (13%), Spain (13%), Germany (12%), France (12%), the Netherlands (12%), Belgium (11%) and Italy (10%).

- The fifth group includes the so-called 'countries of first asylum', which receive massive flows of refugees due to conflicts in a neighbouring country. For example, at the end of 2015, more than one million Syrian and Iraqi refugees were living in Lebanon, representing the equivalent of 20% of its population, and around 400,000 refugees from Sudan were living in Chad (3% of its population).

Small countries have higher proportions of immigrants

With 29% immigrants, Switzerland is ahead of the United States, while the proportion in Luxembourg is even higher (46%). Both the attractiveness and size of the country play a role. The smaller the country, the higher its probable proportion of foreign-born residents. Conversely, the larger the country, the smaller this proportion is likely to be. In 2015, India had 0.4% of immigrants and China 0.07%.

However, if each Chinese province were an independent country – a dozen provinces have more than 50 million inhabitants, and three of them (Guangdong, Shandong, and Henan) have about 100 million – the proportion of immigrants would be much higher, given that migration from province to province, which has increased in scale over recent years, would be counted as international and not internal migration. Conversely, if the European Union formed a single country, the share of immigrants would decrease considerably, since citizens of one EU country living in another would no longer be counted. The relative scale of the two types of migration – internal and international – is thus strongly linked to the way the territory is divided into separate nations.

The number of emigrants is difficult to measure

All immigrants (in-migrants) are also emigrants (out-migrants) from their home countries. Yet the information available for counting emigrants at the level of a particular country is often of poorer quality than for the immigrants,

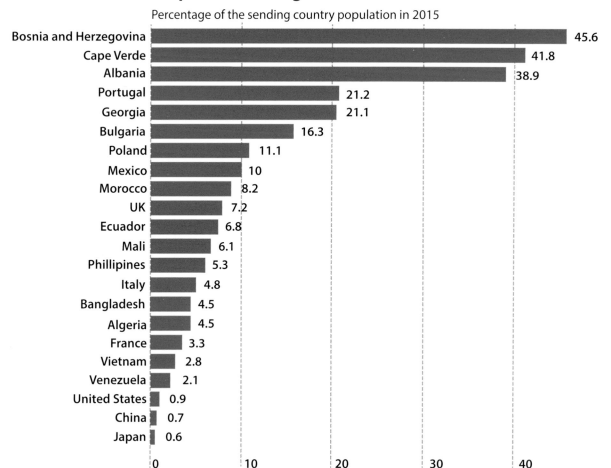

Proportion of emigrants ** in selected countries

Percentage of the sending country population in 2015

Bosnia and Herzegovina	45.6
Cape Verde	41.8
Albania	38.9
Portugal	21.2
Georgia	21.1
Bulgaria	16.3
Poland	11.1
Mexico	10
Morocco	8.2
UK	7.2
Ecuador	6.8
Mali	6.1
Phillipines	5.3
Italy	4.8
Bangladesh	4.5
Algeria	4.5
France	3.3
Vietnam	2.8
Venezuela	2.1
United States	0.9
China	0.7
Japan	0.6

**People born in the country and living abroad

G.Pison, *Population & Societies* no 563, 2019.

even though, at the global level, they represent the same set of people. Countries are probably less concerned about counting their emigrants than their immigrants, given that the former, unlike the latter, are no longer residents and do not use government-funded public services or infrastructure.

However, emigrants often contribute substantially to the economy of their home countries by sending back money and in some cases, they still have the right to vote, which is a good reason for sending countries to track their emigrant population more effectively. The statistical sources are another reason for the poor quality of data on emigrants. Migrant arrivals are better recorded than departures, and the number of emigrants is often estimated based on immigrant statistics in the different host countries.

The number of emigrants varies considerably from one country to another. India headed the list in 2015, with nearly 16 million people born in the country but living in another; Mexico comes in second with more than 12 million emigrants living mainly in the United States. Proportionally, Bosnia and Herzegovina holds a record: there is one Bosnian living abroad for two living in the country, which means that one-third of the people born in Bosnia and Herzegovina have emigrated. Albania is in a similar situation, as well as Cape Verde, an insular country with few natural resources.

Some countries are both immigration and emigration countries. This is the case of the United Kingdom, which had 8.4 million immigrants and 4.7 million emigrants in 2015. The United States has a considerable number of expatriates (2.9 million in 2015), but this is 17 times less in comparison to the number of immigrants (48 million at the same date).

Until recently, some countries have been relatively closed to migration, both inward and outward. This is the case for Japan, which has few immigrants (only 1.7% of its population in 2015) and few emigrants (0.6%).

Immigrants: less than 4% of the world population

According to the United Nations, there were 258 million immigrants in 2017, representing only a small minority of the world population (3.4%); the vast majority of people live in their country of birth. The proportion of immigrants has only slightly increased over recent decades (30 years ago, in 1990, it was 2.9%, and 55 years ago, in 1965, it was 2.3%). It has probably changed only slightly in 100 years.

The four large groups of international migrants, migrant numbers in 2017

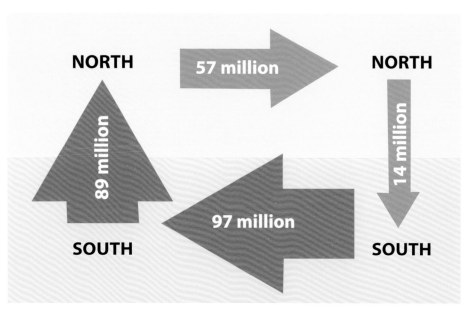

G.Pison, *Population & Societies* no 563, 2019.

Interpretation: In 2017, 14 million people born in the North were living in the South ('North' and 'South' designating, respectively, developed and developing countries)

But the distribution of immigrants is different than it was a century ago. One change is, in the words of Alfred Sauvy, the 'reversal of migratory flows' between North and South, with a considerable share of international migrants now coming from Southern countries.

Today, migrants can be divided into three groups of practically equal size (figure above): migrants born in the South who live in the North (89 million in 2017, according to the United Nations); South-South migrants (97 million), who have migrated from one Southern country to another; and North-North migrants (57 million). The fourth group – those born in the North and who have migrated to the South – was dominant a century ago but is numerically much smaller today (14 million). Despite their large scale, especially in Europe, migrant flows generated since 2015 by conflicts in the Middle East have not significantly changed the global picture of international migration.

13 March 2019

EU immigration to the UK

An estimated 202,000 citizens from other EU countries immigrated to the UK in the year to September 2018, and about 145,000 emigrated abroad. So EU 'net migration' was around 57,000 – roughly the lowest level recorded since 2009.

In the year before the referendum, net EU migration was estimated at 189,000, so there's been a large fall following the vote. We don't know how much of that is a direct result of the decision to leave, but that and the Brexit process over the past few years has clearly had an impact.

Madeleine Sumption, from the Migration Observatory at the University of Oxford, commented:

'The overall story the data tell on EU migration is clear: Britain is not as attractive to EU migrants as it was a couple of years ago. That may be because of Brexit-related political uncertainty, the falling value of the pound making UK wages less attractive, or simply the fact that job opportunities have improved in other EU countries. EU net migration happened to be unusually high in the run-up to the referendum, so at least some of this decline would probably have happened anyway even without Brexit.'

Estimated non-EU net migration, meanwhile, is 261,000 a year – the highest level recorded since 2004. It has been almost consistently higher than EU migration for decades.

Fewer EU citizens are immigrating to the UK, and more are emigrating

The most recent set of figures published cover the year to September 2018.

Since the EU referendum in late June 2016, the estimated number of EU nationals immigrating to the UK fell from 284,000 the year before the vote to 226,000 in the year after. That's now down to 202,000.

Meanwhile the number of EU citizens emigrating has increased from an estimated 95,000 in the year before the referendum to 145,000 now.

The numbers are uncertain

These figures have a margin for error because they're mainly based on surveys of passengers at airports. Net migration from the rest of the EU in any one year could usually be around 30,000 more or less than the estimates.

That means that small changes in immigration from one period to the next might not actually represent what's really happening. With larger changes we can be more certain.

These figures also define immigrants and emigrants as people who change their country of residence for at least

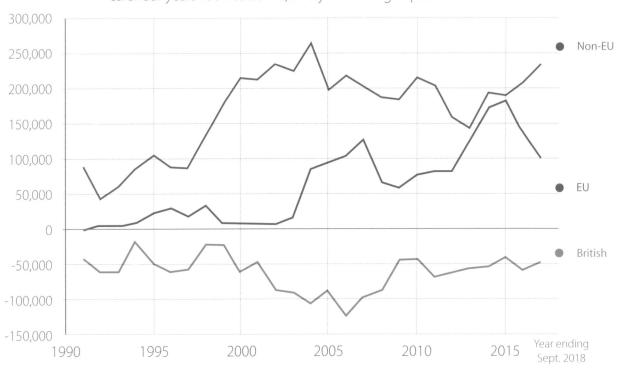

Migration by nationality

Long-term international net migration in the UK by nationality, calendar years 1991 to 2017*, and year ending September 2018

* Figures from 2001-2011 no longer accurate due to revisions, but no alternative available

Source: ONS Long-term International Migration 2016, table 2.01a and Migration Statistics Quarterly Report, February 2019, table 1

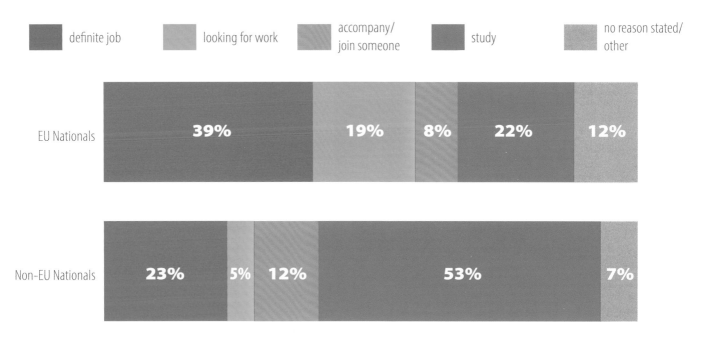

Reasons given for immigrating to the UK
Immigration of EU and non-EU nationals by main reason stated for migrating, year ending September 2018

Legend: definite job | looking for work | accompany/join someone | study | no reason stated/other

EU Nationals: 39% | 19% | 8% | 22% | 12%

Non-EU Nationals: 23% | 5% | 12% | 53% | 7%

* The figures in this chart exclude British nationals. The figures only include the 'main' reason given so the actual proportion coming for any particular reason may be higher.

Source: ONS Provisional Long-Term International Migration estimates, February 2019, table 3

a year – which is called 'long-term migration'. There are separate estimates for the numbers of people who come to the UK for less than a year.

There's been controversy over whether long-term estimates accurately reflect immigration at all.

Reasons for coming here

About four in ten citizens from other EU countries say they come with a definite job lined up. Others usually come looking for work, to study or to join family members in the UK.

Non-EU immigrants, mainly say they come to study.

EU net migration was at historically high levels, but is now falling back

In recent years annual net migration from the rest of the EU has been at historically high levels. In the two years up until September 2016 it was between an estimated 160,000 to 190,000. Back in 2012 it was nearer 70,000 a year.

As the Migration Observatory at the University of Oxford points out, when the EU expanded in 2004, the UK was one of three countries which opened its borders straight away to workers from the new member states.

The new estimates for the year to September 2018 suggest EU net migration has now returned to a level similar to that last seen in 2009.

3.7 million EU citizens in the UK

Around 3.7 million people living in the UK in 2018 were citizens of another EU country. That's about 6% of the UK population, although these figures exclude people who live in communal establishments. Similarly, 6% of the UK population were born in another EU country.

Around 2.3 million nationals of other EU countries are in work, as of October to December 2018.

EU nationals of working age are more likely to be in work than UK nationals and non-EU citizens. About 83% of working age EU citizens in the UK are in work, compared to around 76% of UK nationals and 66% of people from outside the EU.

1.3 million people from the UK live in the rest of the EU

Figures for 2017 suggest that 1.3 million people born in the UK live in other EU countries. We've previously looked at all the estimates in detail.

18 March 2019

Brits abroad: how many people from the UK live in other EU countries?

1.3 million people born in the UK live in other EU countries, according to 2017 estimates from the United Nations (UN). Around 900,000 UK citizens were long-term residents in other EU countries in 2010 and 2011, according to census data across the EU collated by the Office for National Statistics (ONS).

There are two alternative estimates, and neither is perfect

Recent figures on Brits abroad have been compiled by both the UN and the ONS. Both are based mainly on census data gathered from EU countries in 2010 and 2011. The difference between them lies in what's been done to those numbers.

The ONS looks at both UK-born people and UK citizens. It brings together mainly census figures from across the EU from 2010 and 2011. The figures just cover people who live abroad for at least a year, rather than just short-term emigrants.

The UN looks just at UK-born people. It takes the census figures as a starting point and then 'ages' the figures a few years up to 2017, estimating how many people have immigrated to and emigrated from those countries during that period.

The UN data isn't a perfect measure, as different countries define 'immigrant' differently. Some define their migrant population as those born abroad; others count foreign

UK citizens living in the rest of the EU

Number of British citizens living in other EU member states, 2011

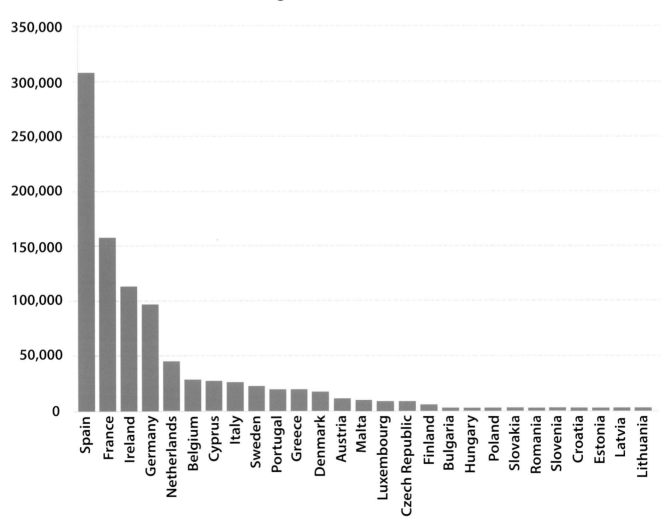

Source: ONS estimates from 'What information is there on British migrants living in Europe?' 2017

citizens. As the House of Commons Library comments, this is an 'unavoidable limitation' of using these figures to compare countries.

So the UN estimate is more up-to-date; the ONS estimate is more certain.

In the context of the Brexit debate, the figures on citizenship are arguably more relevant. That's because free movement rules are based on which country you're a citizen of, rather than where you're born.

Where UK citizens lived in 2010 and 2011

Spain hosts the largest group of UK citizens living in the rest of the EU at an estimated 309,000. France is second with 157,000 and Ireland next with 112,000.

Where UK-born people lived in 2017

Spain is again top of the list: an estimated 310,000 UK-born people lived there in 2017. Ireland is second with 280,000 and France third with 190,000.

UK-born people living in the rest of the EU

Number of UK-born people living in other EU member states, 2017 estimates

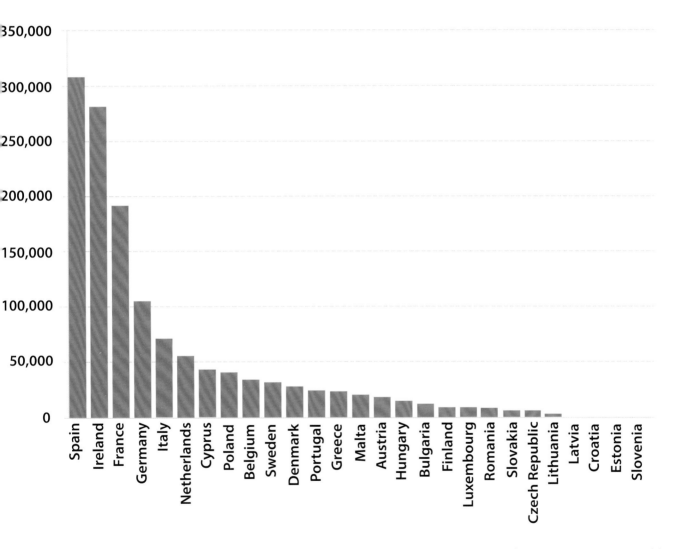

Source: United Nations, 'Trends in International Migrant Stock: Migrants by Destination and Origin', 2017 revision, table 1

Expats across the EU

Estimated size of expat population across the EU, by country of nationality, 2017 estimates

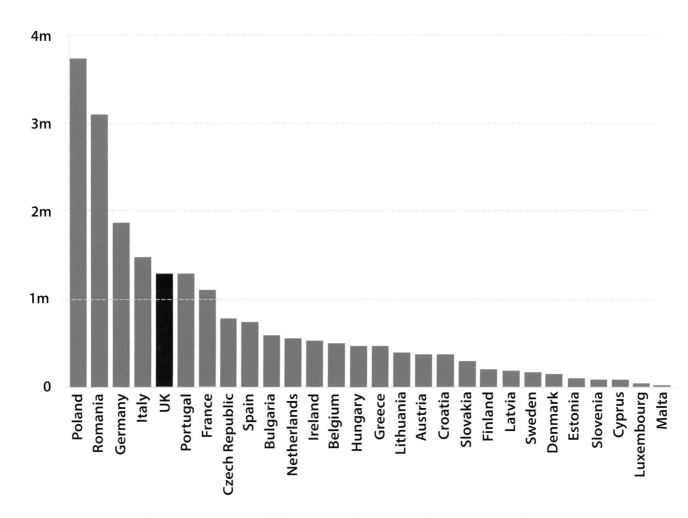

Source: United Nations, 'Trends in International Migrant Stock: Migrants by Destination and Origin', 2017 revision, table 1

Those 1.3 million people place the UK fifth among EU countries for the size of their expat population in other EU member countries.

Poland has the most: an estimated 3.7 million Poles live elsewhere in the EU. Romania, Germany and Italy also have higher expat populations than the UK.

The University of Oxford's Migration Observatory produced similar research in 2011, which has since been updated.

Previous estimates have placed the figure higher, but these aren't the best or most recently available figures

An older estimate by the IPPR think tank estimated that 1.8 million UK nationals lived in other EU countries for at least a year in 2008. This rose to 2.2 million when including people who lived abroad for at least part of the year.

This was produced before all the census data used by the UN was available, so the researchers filled in the gaps using various assumptions.

This estimate was used by the Government, but the IPPR itself no longer uses it. It has more recently used the UN figures.

1 February 2018

More than 750 million people around the world would migrate if they could

By Johnny Wood

Have you ever considered moving permanently to a new country? If the answer is yes, you're far from alone. A new poll reveals that 15% of the global population – over 750 million people – would migrate if they could.

While conflict, famine and natural disasters have driven many people from their homelands, there are also many other reasons for seeking a new life elsewhere, including economic opportunity.

A recent Gallup World Poll survey reveals that the desire to migrate has increased in developed regions like North America and non-EU member states in Europe.

Who's on the move?

In North America, the number of people favouring a move has risen dramatically in the last few years from 10 to 14% since the 2013–2016 period. Despite a strengthening jobs market, 16% of those surveyed in the US in 2017 told Gallup they wanted to live abroad, the highest increase recorded by the poll.

In the European Union – where citizens have the right to freedom of movement – the desire to migrate has remained unchanged since 2012 at 21%, while attitudes to moving in non-EU European states have stabilised recently following a rise at the start of the decade.

Desire to migrate up worldwide

Ideally, if you had the opportunity, would you like to move PERMANENTLY to another country, or would you prefer to continue living in this country?

	2010-2012 %	2013-2016 %	2015-2017 %
Sub-Saharan Africa	30	31	33
Latin America and Caribbean	18	23	27
Europe (non-European Union)	21	27	26
Middle East and North Africa	19	22	24
European Union	20	21	21
Commonwealth of Independent States	15	14	15
Northern America	10	10	14
Australia/New Zealand/Oceania	9	10	9
East Asia	8	7	8
South Asia	8	8	8
Southeast Asia	7	7	7
World	13	14	15

Note: Figures represent precentage who would like to move if they could

GALLUP WORLD POLL

People in refugee hotspots continue to hope for a better future in another country. The poll shows the number wanting to move rising in Latin America and the Caribbean, the Middle East and North Africa, and sub-Saharan Africa, where ongoing armed conflicts, for example in Sudan, Syria and Yemen, are fuelling the desire to migrate.

In poor countries from Haiti to Albania well over half of the citizens expressed a wish to move. The poll showed that 71% of the Sierra Leone population wanted to leave.

Where do migrants want to live?

The US remains the leading choice for would-be migrants and this has been the case since Gallup's polls began over a decade ago. Despite the Trump administration toughening immigration rules, one in five migrants chose the US as their favoured destination in 2017.

Top desired destinations for potential migrants

To which country would you like to move?

	2010-2012 %	2013-2016 %	Estimated number of adults (in millions)
United States	22	21	158
Canada	6	6	47
Germany	4	6	42
France	5	5	36
Australia	4	5	36
United Kingdom	7	4	34
Saudi Arabia	5	3	24
Spain	4	3	21
Japan	2	2	17
Italy	3	2	15

GALLUP WORLD POLL

Across the border, Canada is in second place – the top choice of 47 million potential migrants. Germany, in third, was the preferred destination for 42 million.

Interest in the UK has dropped in recent years, with uncertainty related to the 2016 Brexit vote a potential factor.

According to UN figures, high-income countries attract the majority of international migrants, a trend accounting for 64% of the global total in 2017.

2 January 2019

Boris Johnson's dramatic immigration u-turn leaves 2.5 million uncertain of their future

THE CONVERSATION

An article from **The Conversation.**

By Adrienne Young Lecturer at The City Law School, City, University of London

Less than a month after Boris Johnson officially became the UK's prime minister, his government has announced changes to the status of EU citizens after the current deadline for UK withdrawal from the EU – 31 October 2019.

The new home secretary, Priti Patel, has said that if the UK leaves the EU without a deal on that day, then free movement will end immediately for all EU citizens in the UK.

This has caused much anxiety and confusion among the almost 3.5 million EU citizens in the UK – 2.5 million of whom have not yet registered for settled status, having been given a deadline of 2020 to get it done.

The previous government, led by Theresa May, made very different promises to these people. They were told that the UK wanted to 'guarantee the rights of EU citizens who are already living in Britain … as early as we can.' It appears that the new government has gone back on this promise.

EU citizens are still welcome to visit the UK for short trips without a visa. However, anyone planning to stay long-term after 31 October will be subject to proposed new rules if the UK leaves without a deal. So what is being planned by the new government in case of a no-deal for EU citizens?

Change of plan

Ending free movement on 31 October means that there would be no grace period for anyone who arrived after this date. A previous transition period was set to last until 31 December 2020. During this time, EU citizens arriving after

Brexit day would enjoy the same rights as those who were there before.

Now, EU citizens would be subject to the planned new immigration system immediately.

The Department of Health has also said that after 31 October 2019, without a deal, NHS trusts will have to start to charge EU citizens for previously free treatment. This would mean NHS trusts would need to check the immigration status of EU citizens seeking treatment. This proposal has already been criticised by the British Medical Association. It would add more work to an NHS already under great strain.

Aside from anything else, the plan has been criticised for being impractical. The previous government admitted in January 2019 there needed to be some time between the end of freedom of movement and a new immigration system coming into force. This is because it would be difficult for employers, universities, landlords and others to distinguish between pre-exit residents and post-withdrawal arrivals. In particular, businesses have said it will make it difficult for them to recruit workers.

What do EU citizens need to do now?

The advice from the Home Office to EU citizens wanting to stay in the UK beyond 31 October is to apply for settled or pre-settled status under its EU Settlement Scheme. This has been officially open since 30 March, 2019. However, there are some concerns about this, too.

Just over 1 million applicants have already been granted settlement under this scheme. That's approximately 30% of the eligible population.

For those who have already applied or who are in the UK before 31 October, there should be no problem. However, there will probably be disruption for those who arrive after November 1. They will not be eligible to apply for settlement.

There will also be disruption for those who do not apply for EU settlement in time (and there is not much time left) and want to change jobs or move house after Brexit. Employers and landlords would be required to check these individuals' immigration statuses, and it could be difficult to distinguish if they arrived before or after withdrawal.

There are serious concerns around certain groups of vulnerable individuals who will have most difficulty applying successfully for EU settlement, such as children without a passport, women in abusive relationships or those who simply cannot read English.

Of the approximately 3.5 million EU citizens in the UK, there are still 2.5 million who have yet to apply for EU settlement. It is unclear how many of them are vulnerable. I have previously highlighted that if large numbers of individuals become illegally resident after a certain cut-off date (for example, if free movement ends on 31 October) anyone who does not have settled status but is still in the UK then could be illegal, and expelled automatically.

Furthermore, this could affect British citizens in the EU. The current arrangement for this group of approximately 1.3m people is based on reciprocity. But ending free movement on October 31 would mean British citizens in the EU would also lose their rights to stay in the EU. In the rush to end free movement as soon as possible, rights of British citizens in the EU seem to have been forgotten.

Another Windrush?

A leaked Home Office discussion document has already noted that it would be practically difficult to enforce an immediate end to free movement because of various complexities in establishing the system. In particular, it warned of a repeat of the Windrush scandal.

While the end to free movement will only become reality if the UK leaves the EU without a deal on the newest deadline of 31 October, the deadlock between the EU and the UK suggests a growing likelihood of no-deal – especially under Boris Johnson's new government. It is cold comfort for EU citizens in the UK and British citizens in the EU that once again citizens appear to be the bargaining chips for negotiations between the EU and the UK.

22 August 2019

What's the impact of immigration, according to Europeans and Americans?

Migration is seen as a blessing for cuisine, but also a catalyst for crime.

By Tanya Abraham

With immigration becoming a more pressing national issue in recent years, a new YouGov survey conducted in seven European nations and the United States has sought to find out exactly what citizens believe to be the impact of migrants on their country – for good and ill.

Food, culture and sport are the top areas to benefit from immigration

In all countries except France, the most commonly agreed benefit of immigration has been better food. This figure was highest in the US, Norway and Britain, where around half of people (between 47% and 50%) think migrants have had a positive impact on cuisine.

Migrants' contribution to the national culture is also widely acknowledged, being the second most frequently mentioned benefit of immigration in most nations (and third in the US and fourth in Germany). Again Americans, Britons and Norwegians are the most likely to feel their nations have benefited in this way at between 39% and 42%, along with 38% of Swedes.

In contrast to the other nations, the French are most likely to see the biggest benefit of immigration to have been on sport, at 32%. Alongside the Germans, they are, however, the least likely to be able to name any benefits of immigration, with only half (between 51% and 52%) being able to put their finger on anything that migration has made better in their country.

What do Europeans and Americans most commonly see as being the benefits of immigration?

Which, if any, of the following do you think has benefited from immigration in the country?
(Please tick all that apply) % Top three most popular responses in each country shown

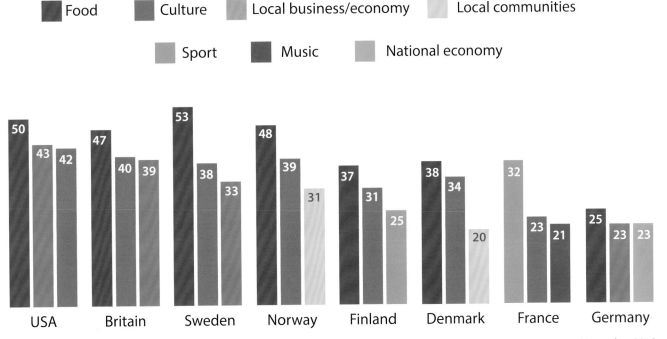

Food Culture Local business/economy Local communities

Sport Music National economy

	USA	Britain	Sweden	Norway	Finland	Denmark	France	Germany
	50	47	53	48	37	38	32	25
	43	40	38	39	31	34	23	23
	42	39	33	31	25	20	21	23

yougov.com

15-25 November 2018

Crime is the most negative outcome of immigration

The most commonly given downside of immigration is increased crime, coming top of the list in five of the countries we surveyed and second or third in the others. It is especially likely to be cited in Denmark, Sweden, Germany and Norway (at between 62% and 68%).

People are also consistently worried about the impact immigrants have on national security (between 31% and 62%) and their country's welfare systems (between 33% and 48%).

Costs versus benefits overall

Looking at combined answers to the positive and negative aspects of immigration reveals that one in four Americans (30%) believe it only brings benefits, making them the most pro-immigration nation. Britain comes a distant second in this regard, on 22%.

By contrast, 37% of Germans were only able to name negative consequences of immigration, making them the most sceptical of the countries. They are followed by France, Finland and Denmark where around a third (31-33%) likewise have nothing good to say about immigration.

What do Europeans and Americans most commonly see as being the harms of immigration?

Which, if any, of the following do you think has been harmed by from immigration in the country?
(Please tick all that apply) % Top three most popular responses in each country shown

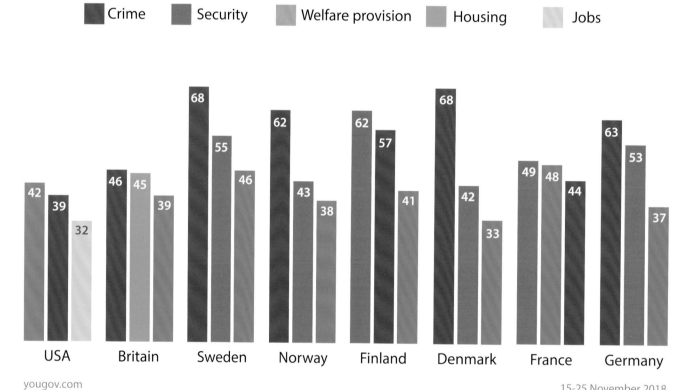

■ Crime ■ Security ■ Welfare provision ■ Housing ■ Jobs

yougov.com   15-25 November 2018

In Britain and Sweden people are more likely than those in other nations to see a negative impact on housing (between 44% and 45%) and healthcare (between 36% and 37%, alongside 39% of French people).

The impact on jobs is also a bigger concern in Britain and France (29% each) and the US (32%) than elsewhere.

The proportion of people who gave at least one negative impact of immigration is higher in all countries than the number who were able to give a positive one – except in the US where 71% could name something good that immigrants have done, compared to 65% who could point at something bad.

This identifies the extent of the most die-hard groups on immigration. A further question looked at the more nuanced picture of whether people found the overall impact of immigration tended to be more positive or more negative. The nations split into three groups.

The first (France, Germany, Denmark, Finland and Sweden) are more likely to say that immigration has generally had a negative overall impact, and by wide margins. The Germans in particular feel immigration has been broadly bad for their country – 53% say this compared to just 18% who feel the opposite.

The second group, into which Britain and Norway fall, are split. In Britain, 39% think immigration's impact has been more bad than good compared to 37% who think it has been more good than bad. In Finland these figures are 32% and 34%, respectively.

Alone in the final group is the United States, where people are in fact more likely to believe that immigration has been better for the country than not, at 39% compared to 33% who take the negative view.

13 June 2019

Britons and Americans are the most likely to think immigration has benefited their country more than it has harmed it

On balance, do you think immigration has benefited or harmed the country more, or is it neither? % of people in each country

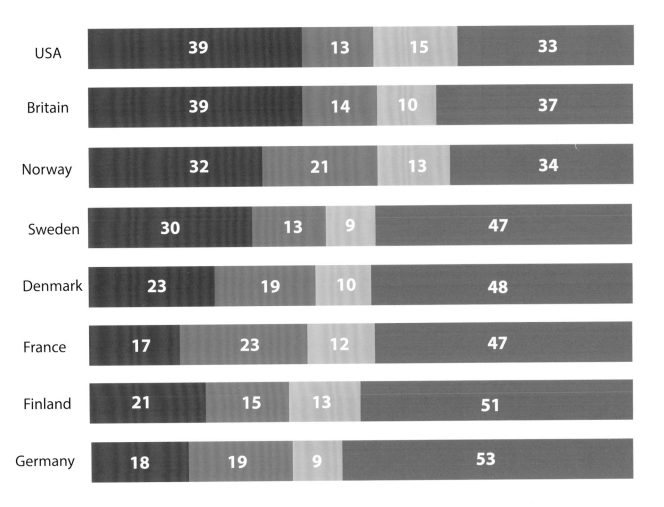

- ■ Generally benefited the country more
- ■ It has neither benefited nor harmed the country
- ■ Don't know
- ■ Generally harmed the country more

Country	Benefited	Neither	Don't know	Harmed
USA	39	13	15	33
Britain	39	14	10	37
Norway	32	21	13	34
Sweden	30	13	9	47
Denmark	23	19	10	48
France	17	23	12	47
Finland	21	15	13	51
Germany	18	19	9	53

yougov.com

15-25 November 2018

EU migrant workers in key occupations

Key occupations with highest share of EU migrant workers

42%
Packers, bottlers, canners and fillers

40%
Food, drink and tobacco process operatives

34%
Weighers, graders and sorters

27%
Vehicle valeters and cleaners

29%
Cleaning and housekeeping managers and supervisors

Source: IPPR *Striking the right deal: UK-EU migration and the Brexit negotiations*

www.ippr.org

Study estimates 500,000 EU workers are in low-skilled UK jobs

Migration Observatory report says employers could struggle to find workers to fill roles after Brexit

By Lisa O'Carroll

An estimated 500,000 EU citizens are working in low-skilled jobs in the UK such as picking fruit, cleaning offices, working in warehouses and food factories, a report by leading academics has found.

The report by the Migration Observatory at the University of Oxford said that employers could struggle to find workers after Brexit and the risk of labour exploitation might be heightened under the two main options available to companies to find staff willing to do the work once freedom of movement ends.

In the most extensive analysis of the jobs EU nationals are filling, Migration Observatory found 132,000 in elementary cleaning jobs, 120,000 in basic hospitality jobs such as coffee shops, 96,000 in warehouses, 91,000 in factory plants and 26,000 on building sites.

Another 89,000 were truck, van and taxi drivers; 82,000 worked in care services; 74,000 working in food processing; 68,000 as shop assistants and 54,000 in other administrative jobs.

The vast majority of the estimated 3.6 million to 3.8 million EU citizens in the country were in skilled jobs with 537,000 in 'high-skilled jobs' with degree or equivalent qualifications.

Another 616,000 were in upper- to middle-skilled jobs with school plus substantial training with 781,000 in lower-middle skilled jobs defined as those involving school qualifications and 'some training'.

Low skilled jobs defined as 'requiring only compulsory schooling' were taken up by 503,000 EU citizens compared to 2.4 million British citizens.

The Government has said it wants to extend an existing youth mobility scheme for Australians, Canadians and other specified non-EU countries including Japan and Monaco to allow them work in these low-skilled jobs.

But Madeleine Sumption, director of the Migration Observatory, said this would not be sufficient.

'There's no guarantee that youth mobility can provide staff for unpalatable roles in out-of-the-way places.

'That's because the scheme gives workers lots of options, and people with options often prefer to work in shops and bars rather than muddy fields or food processing plants.'

With virtual full employment in the UK, employers are concerned they will be left high and dry after Brexit if the Government does not come up with a scheme for low-skilled workers.

One potential way to ensure a continued supply of labour after free movement from European countries ends on the UK's departure from the EU would be to allow businesses to sponsor visas for low-skilled workers. But such schemes had 'significant drawbacks', the Migration Observatory report said.

Sumption also said that employer-sponsored schemes would limit workers to one job and would not prevent exploitation.

Her view was echoed by the anti-trafficking charity Focus on Labour Exploitation.

'The UK already has one of the weakest labour law enforcement structures in Europe, which means abusive employers are often able to operate with impunity. Increased restrictions on immigration and removal of the right to work for EU nationals will place yet more workers at risk of exploitation,' said the director, Caroline Robinson.

A Home Office spokesman said: 'After we leave the EU, we will have in place an immigration system which works in the best interests of the whole of the UK.

'This system will be based on evidence. The Government has commissioned advice from the migration advisory committee and we continue to engage with a range of stakeholders.'

30 August 2018

Migrants and the media: what shapes the narratives on immigration in different countries

An article from **The Conversation.**

THE CONVERSATION

By Rob McNeil, Researcher, Centre on Migration Policy and Society (COMPAS), Deputy Director, Migration Observatory, University of Oxford

If you want to spoil a movie for yourself, wait for a nice dramatic moment and then imagine what it was like to shoot it: the cameras, sound and lighting crews all around; the portable toilets round the back; the half-finished bowl of crisps on the catering table. If a film is to succeed, it needs us to suspend our disbelief and not think about the process.

But when we consume news media, we need to do the opposite – and think carefully about how and why these products were made. When it comes to reporting on polarising and contentious issues such as migration, what happens behind the scenes in media organisations can affect not only how we think about the issue, but even policy itself.

Our team of researchers from the University of Oxford's Centre on Migration, Policy and Society (COMPAS), the Budapest Business School and the European Journalism Centre based at Maastricht in the Netherlands, has been working to turn the camera around on news production in Europe. Our objective was to understand why different themes and narratives about migration have taken hold in different countries – and what factors contributed to the people creating these stories operating so differently.

We interviewed more than 200 journalists and key media sources (such as government migration spokespeople, NGOs and think tanks) in nine EU countries, looking at their personal reasons for working the way they did and the institutional, social and political norms that shaped their outputs.

For example – compare this Swedish newspaper reporter who is very positive about the role of journalism: "I enjoy great respect. People listen to what I say and want to hear my opinion", with this UK newspaper journalist: "Even my own friends hate the fact that I work here and think I'm a disgrace, but I've just learned to ignore it and I just get on with my work."

The same two journalists articulate very different ways of reporting migration. The Swedish journalist describes their approach to reporting on non-EU migrants who are not fleeing persecution or seeking asylum:

> *'Globalisation is a positive force. We rarely write something negative. Labour force migration is positive.'*

Contrast with this the UK journalist's explanation of how they would use the term 'migrant', in general:

> *'To be brutally honest, it's more likely to be people who are a burden on society than those who are a benefit to society, because there is more newsworthiness in a foreign criminal or a teenager who's being looked after by the council than, say, a brilliant academic who's come here to further their career … so from our perspective it's more newsworthy if people are abusing the system or exploiting loopholes or abusing the hospitality being extended to them by British society … because that triggers a reaction in readers.'*

Both reporters work for newspapers and both cover the issue of migration, but they describe very differently both the place they occupy in society, and the subject they report on.

Matter of perception

Reporting is a fundamentally human process – ideas, data and anecdotes all pass through reporters, whose perceptions of the world, areas of interest and biases are all affected by various national, social, institutional and political factors. Some are obvious and affect their immediate working experience – such as what they imagine their proprietor or editor might want to read or see. Others are more abstract –

EVERYONE IS WELCOME

such as their sense of responsibility to help people, or to 'tell it like it is, warts and all'. This can have a big impact on the reporting of a sensitive issue such as immigration.

These sometimes competing pressures affect everything from what a reporter perceives will actually constitute a valid story, to the words they will use to tell that story. For example, here is a Hungarian broadcast journalist talking about the importance of terminology to the immigration debate:

'We prefer to use the term 'refugee', as the word 'migrant' might sound correct in English, but in Hungarian a 'migrant' is an enemy who will kill us. Therefore, we call them 'refugees'… We could use the term 'migrant', but it is a delicate one as it is widely used by pro-government propaganda.'

This national context is critical. Different media traditions are contingent on national history: experiences of migration differ from country to country and even norms of the role of journalism can be fundamentally different.

In Spain and Italy we found it common for reporters to highlight the expectation that they should make an emotional connection with the reader. In Germany and Sweden there was more focus on technical reporting. In some states with a recent history of autocratic government – such as Hungary – there was a more obvious effort by governments to try to influence reporting than in more established democracies.

But government influence was also felt in more nebulous and indirect ways in some countries where the ideal of press freedom was highly prized. Personal connections between politicians and powerful individuals within media organisations are known and understood by reporters, who consider this when they choose how to report issues. One UK newspaper journalist said the owner of the paper was always in their mind when reporting on a story: 'There is an awareness of the owner's circle of friends – he knows lots of influential people – and [awareness of] his enemies.'

Perhaps the most important takeaway is that journalists both shape – and are shaped by – their national policy discourse on migration. Reporters consider, of course, the factual question of 'what has happened?', but other variables also shape the world in which they operate: including what their audiences expect, how the story has been reported by other media, what may get the reporter into trouble, what the editor thinks of the issue and what sells.

Press culture

The way different national media report migration both emerges from cultural practices within media organisations, but also reinforces them.

This can have profound impacts on policy outcomes. For example, the culture within UK media – particularly within newspapers – is particularly focused on winning political victories. Would the Brexit referendum result have been the same if it was more moderate?

German journalists, on the other hand, were particularly focused on moderation and social justice. The country may have reacted differently to receiving a million asylum seekers if the nation's media had been less homogenous in this approach.

Finally, Hungary has developed a 'patron and client' model of government relations with media. Would the administration of Victor Orban, the prime minister, have been able to implement its radical anti-immigration policies if the media were less dependent on government and had a greater degree of editorial freedom?

These questions are hypothetical, of course. But by drawing attention to the process of media production, rather than just content, we highlight the need for thoughtful scrutiny of media practices, that may, in turn help lead to better understanding of media and its role within policymaking in the future.

26 April 2019

New poll shows British people have become more positive about immigration

An article from The Conversation.

By Bobby Duffy, Visiting Senior Research Fellow, King's College London

THE CONVERSATION

Michael Gove, the British environment secretary, sparked a heated debate when he said recently: 'Britain has the most liberal attitude towards migration of any European country. And that followed the Brexit vote.'

His implication that the Brexit vote was a force for a more positive view of immigration in Britain has been vigorously challenged by some.

And you can see why it might grate: analysis by King's College London shows that media coverage of immigration tripled in the campaign, and was 'overwhelmingly negative'.

But Gove is right to say that people in Britain are now more positive about immigration, as shown by new polling released by Ipsos MORI, tracking attitudes towards immigration after the recent Windrush scandal.

Gove cited an Ipsos survey from the end of 2017, which does indeed show that from the ten European countries included, Britain is most likely to think immigration has had a positive effect on the country.

A more recent European Commission survey across all 28 EU countries shows that, while the UK is not quite top, it is the third most likely to say that immigration is an opportunity rather than a problem, behind only Sweden and Ireland.

And this is a shift that can't be explained purely by the weight of negative media coverage of immigration dying down after the referendum.

I've been reviewing immigration attitudes for nearly 20 years, and I'm really not used to seeing Britain at the top of any league table of immigration positivity: this is something new.

Picking out European countries...

Would you say that immigration has generally had a positive or negative impact on your country?

2017 – Very positive/Fairly positive

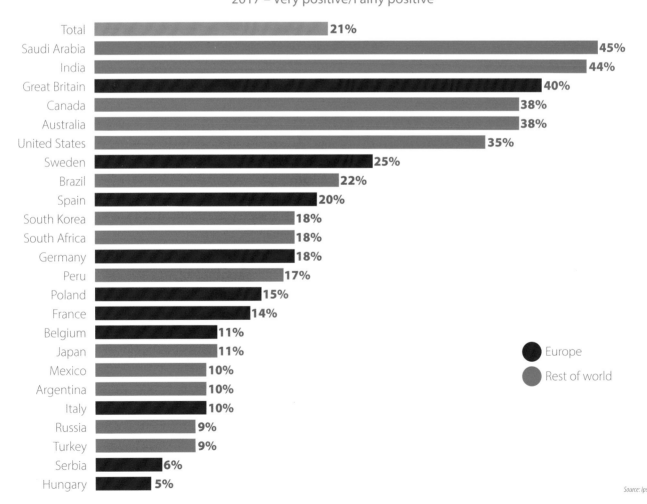

Country	%
Total	21%
Saudi Arabia	45%
India	44%
Great Britain	40%
Canada	38%
Australia	38%
United States	35%
Sweden	25%
Brazil	22%
Spain	20%
South Korea	18%
South Africa	18%
Germany	18%
Peru	17%
Poland	15%
France	14%
Belgium	11%
Japan	11%
Mexico	10%
Argentina	10%
Italy	10%
Russia	9%
Turkey	9%
Serbia	6%
Hungary	5%

● Europe
● Rest of world

Source: Ipsos MORI

Britain moves up, Sweden down, rest negative but stable...

% saying immigration's impact on their country has been *Very/Fairly positive*

Great Britain   **Sweden**   Spain

Germany   France   **Italy**

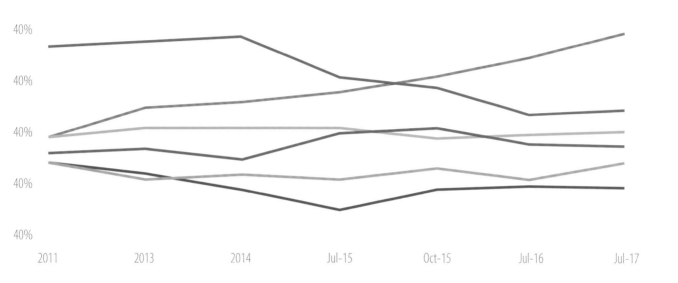

40%						
40%						
40%						
40%						
40%						

2011   2013   2014   Jul-15   Oct-15   Jul-16   Jul-17

Source: Ipsos MORI

As the chart above shows, positive attitudes have doubled in Britain since 2011, while they've flatlined at a low level in most other countries, or fallen in the case of Sweden.

And a new survey published by Ipsos MORI shows this trend remains stable. The switch from a negative balance of opinion to a positive one started before the 2016 referendum on EU membership, in the middle of 2015 – but it did gain pace after.

Reassurance and regret

There are two broad explanations for why this is happening – that the change is being driven by 'reassurance', or 'regret'.

The first is the idea that people feel they can now say that immigration has positive aspects, because numbers are coming down, or they believe numbers will be lower in the future, as a result of Brexit.

Regret, on the other hand, could be driven by a realisation of what we're losing from lower immigration: as numbers fall and warnings of skills shortages and economic impacts increase, the extent to which the country benefits from immigration becomes more obvious.

Clearly these are simplifications – there are other explanations and these are not mutually exclusive views. But in our latest survey, we tried to assess the balance between these two explanations for the first time, by simply asking people why they are more positive.

And as the chart on page 24 shows, there is an almost perfect balance between the two explanations: around four in ten say they're more aware of the contribution that immigrants make, and the same proportion say they're reassured numbers are falling or will fall.

Of those who have become more positive, people are split – four in five say it's because they recognise contribution of immigrants and same proportion say it's because they are reassured that numbers are reducing

Some people's opinions on immigration have shifted since the vote to leave the EU. Which of the following, if any, apply to your views? You can choose as many as you like.

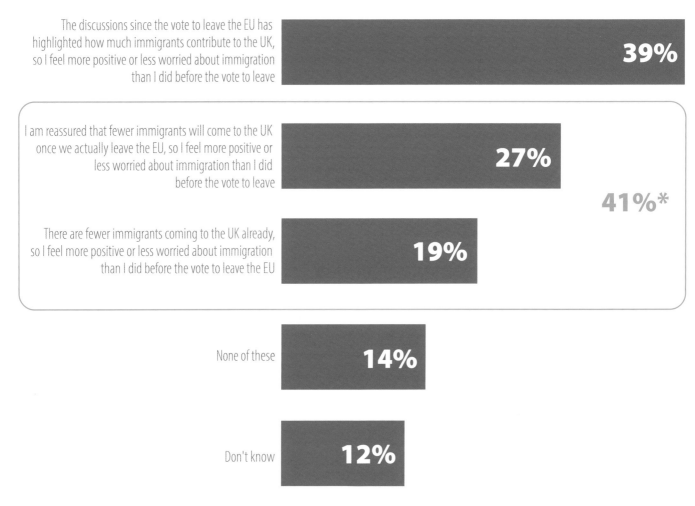

The discussions since the vote to leave the EU has highlighted how much immigrants contribute to the UK, so I feel more positive or less worried about immigration than I did before the vote to leave — **39%**

I am reassured that fewer immigrants will come to the UK once we actually leave the EU, so I feel more positive or less worried about immigration than I did before the vote to leave — **27%**

41%*

There are fewer immigrants coming to the UK already, so I feel more positive or less worried about immigration than I did before the vote to leave the EU — **19%**

None of these — **14%**

Don't know — **12%**

Base: All who say they have become more positive about immigration since EU Referendum (218)
*People selecting either one of these options

Source: Ipsos MORI

An emotive debate

As with so much about immigration attitudes, there is no one clear answer or view, and therefore no clear indication for future policy and political direction. The very real trends of increased positivity actually give the Government little clue as to whether they should loosen their drive to control numbers, or stick to their guns on the 'hostile environment"'immigration policy that has come in for so much criticism in recent months.

Immigration is well recognised as a polarising issue, and one of the key topics in a referendum vote that split the country down the middle.

But what's more often missed is that our views are also full of nuance and contradiction. There are not just two immovable and monolithic pro- and anti-immigration blocs, as shown by our previous research, and another of our just-released polls for the *Evening Standard*. For example, the majority of the public would like to see the Government's cap on the number of doctors coming to the UK from outside the EU lifted entirely or increased – but the majority support the cap, or even greater restrictions, on computer scientists.

One thing seems clear – British people's more positive outlook seems to be little to do with the Brexit debate leading people to be better informed on immigration facts, at least on key aspects like the scale of immigration. When we asked what percentage of the population immigrants make up, which we've done regularly over many years, the average guess was 28%, compared with a reality of around 13%: we are just as wrong as we've always been.

Of course, this is because our emotions colour our views of scale as much as the other way round. The immigration debate remains an emotive one, caught up in our identity, culture and values more than cold calculations.

But all these challenges don't mean that attitudes to immigration should be ignored in setting immigration policy. There is a case that Brexit was partly a result of ignoring immigration concerns, rather than either acting to reassure people, or challenging their views.

With a white paper on the post-Brexit immigration system now expected by July, the risk for the Government comes not from listening to apparently fickle and contradictory public opinion, it comes from mishearing or caricaturing it – again.

26 May 2018

Immigration and the challenge of identity

Immigration is a fact of life in our globalized world. But how can newcomers maintain their cultural identities in an era of Trump and Brexit?

By Tania Bagan

Can immigrants maintain their identities and traditions in their new homes? Or should they assimilate fully to ensure peaceful co-existence with their hosts, speaking only the local language and abiding by local customs?

These questions have taken on new importance as large numbers of immigrants – drawn to economic opportunities or driven from their homes by conflict and human rights abuses – ebb and flow across the globe, stirring resentment and a nationalist backlash in some countries.

Four university students, including three living in countries far from their birthplaces, addressed immigration, assimilation and identity in a recent News-Decoder webinar.

Arjun Balasundarum, from India, and Christine Fernando, whose parents were born in Sri Lanka, spoke from Indiana University, while Kit Keene, an American studying in London, and Arsentiy Novak, born in Ukraine, represented King's College London.

'The fear among immigrants in the US is something very real.'

Each of the News-Decoder student panellists is living in a country that in the past year has voted in favour of policies that are radically at odds with the liberal economic and social orthodoxy that has prevailed in Western society since World War Two.

Balasundarum and Fernando are in the United States, where President Donald Trump presides over a nation more divided than ever, where a large gap has opened up between right-wing nationalists favouring curbs in immigrants, and politically-correct urban dwellers.

Keene and Novak are in Britain, which is struggling to come to terms with its surprise vote last year to leave the European Union and the implications of that decision on the free movement of labour and immigration.

Balasundarum spoke of the political climate under Trump. 'Though the current administration is just focusing on undocumented immigrants, the ones who are here legally still feel threatened. The fear among immigrants in the United States is something very real.'

'Assimilation is a two-way street.'

Fernando addressed the fraught question of whether an immigrant should assimilate the host country's culture and practices, increasing their chances of being accepted but risking the loss of identity.

She underscored the contributions that immigrants can make to the diversity and creativity of the local culture – quite evident, ironically, in both the United States and Britain, where cuisines, shops and traditions from all around the world flourish.

'People assume that people come here and want to fade into monolithic American culture,' Fernando said. 'The U.S. was built on immigrants. If you focus too much on assimilation, you forget how much immigrants contribute and change and create culture.'

Keene, too, felt the responsibility to adapt should not have to fall entirely on the newcomer. 'It's on both the 'natives' and the 'migrants' to integrate a little,' she said. 'People living in a country should accept that their country is changing and that there are new values being brought in that they may need to adapt to.'

Born in Ukraine, Novak decried the atmosphere of political correctness at university that can impede some students from asking questions of others and which can deepen misconceptions by prioritising safety over confrontation.

'With this notion of tolerance, and being presumed to have an understanding of cultures, we are disallowed to critique or speak out against that which we don't like,' Novak said.

For these four students, immigration is a process both of assimilation on the part of the newcomer and of acceptance on the part of the hosts. Ideally, they agreed, it should be a balanced, reciprocal process and not a one-way street.

20 June 2017

Why the world needs more immigration

By Luis Pablo de la Horra

- ◆ Restrictive immigration policies have adverse effects on host economies

- ◆ The long-term impact of immigration on employment is negligible

- ◆ Open borders would substantially reduce global poverty

In his classic work, *The Myth of the Rational Voter*, Bryan Caplan identifies four systematic biases about economics held by the average citizen: make-work bias (an inclination to overestimate the disadvantages of temporary job destruction due to productivity increases), anti-market bias (a tendency to overlook the benefits of the market as a coordination mechanism), pessimistic bias (an inclination to underestimate the present and future performance of the economy), and anti-foreign bias (a tendency to underestimate the economic benefits of interaction with foreigners).

These widespread biases are far from harmless. Wrong ideas held by voters usually lead to catastrophic policies: politicians undertake those policies that they deem popular in order to get reelected. If those policies beget pernicious consequences for the economy, harmless beliefs turn into lower living standards for all.

The most potentially harmful bias is the anti-foreign one. This manifests itself politically in two main ways: protectionism and anti-immigration policies. Despite the recent surge of protectionism in some developed countries, free trade is now the rule rather than the exception in most parts of the world.

But when it comes to immigration, only a few steps have been taken in the direction of liberalisation (even though the consensus about the benefits of more open borders in the economics profession is probably as strong as the consensus around free trade).

Anti-immigration policies, however, reduce the well-being of both potential immigrants and host societies and even a partial liberalisation of restrictions would, in the long-term, improve the standards of living globally.

The economic case against less restrictive immigration policies rests on shaky pillars. The most common arguments are related to the supposedly negative effects that immigration has on the host country's labour market, and more specifically, its impact on employment and wages. According to those in favour of restrictions, immigrants do not only take natives' jobs but they also have a depressive effect on wages.

However, economic theory does not support these assertions. First, the economy is not a zero-sum game: the numbers of jobs available is not finite. As pointed out by Alex Tabarrok (here and here), immigrants are not only producers but also consumers: an increase in demand triggered by the expansion of the immigrant population goes hand in hand with an increase in total employment.

Secondly: contrary to conventional wisdom, it's not only highly qualified immigrants who create positive externalities on host economies. Low-skilled immigrants tend to take lower productivity jobs (as they often either lack higher education or do not speak the language), allowing the native-born to access higher-productivity jobs (assuming a flexible labour market).

Indeed, this is borne out by the evidence. After World War II, the US labour force increased dramatically due to immigration and the massive entry of women into the labour market. It moved from 60 million in 1950 to around 150 million workers in 2007. And yet, the unemployment rate in 2007 was as low as 4.6 per cent, near full employment.

The same logic also applies to wages. The law of supply and demand says that an increase in the supply of labour would inevitably cause lower wages. However, more immigrants also generate a higher demand for goods and services, which results in a higher demand for labour, thus preventing a generalised decrease in salaries. Even in those cases when wages in a particular sector are temporarily pushed down, lower wages lead to lower costs for companies, which usually results in lower prices for consumers.

Immigration-friendly policies are also useful when it comes to tackling the demographic problem that many developed countries are experiencing. The progressive ageing of the American population is already having a deleterious impact on the US social security system.

According to the Population Reference Bureau, the number of Americans over 65 years old will have increased from 15 per cent in 2014 to 24 per cent of the population by 2060. As a result, the worker-to-beneficiary ratio will decrease by 32 per cent, from 3.4 in 1990 to 2.3 in 2030. This could be mitigated by adopting a more flexible immigration policy to increase the working population, reversing the trend that will otherwise end up with significant spending cuts in social security benefits.

Indeed, this benefit directly contradicts one of the other strongly held views about immigrants: that they pose a burden on the host economy. Their net fiscal impact (defined as taxes paid by immigrants minus public services and benefits received) is thought to be overwhelmingly negative when compared with the fiscal impact of natives. Yet the evidence does not support this idea. As pointed out in 2011, a survey paper on the economic effects of immigration, Sari Pekkala Kerr and William R. Kerr stated:

'It is very clear that the net social impact of an immigrant over his or her lifetime depends substantially and in predictable ways on the immigrants' age at arrival, education, reason for migration, and similar […] The estimated net fiscal impact of migrants also varies substantially across studies, but the overall magnitudes relative to the GDP remain modest […] The more credible analyses typically find small fiscal effects.'

Therefore, there are no good reasons to impose tough restrictions on labour mobility in the name of fiscal sustainability.

Nor is immigration just of benefit to the host countries. Immigrants usually send a portion of their income back home with the aim of economically supporting their families and friends there. These remittances are flows of capital from developed to developing countries that vastly assist in the economic development of the home country.

But the main beneficiaries of eliminating barriers to labour mobility are, of course, immigrants themselves. This is due to the concept of Place Premium. This concept, first introduced by Michael Clemens, Claudio E. Montenegro and Lant Pritchettin in a 2008 paper, refers to the automatic increase in earnings (PPP adjusted) that a worker experiences by moving from a low-productivity country to a high-productivity country, without increasing the worker's human capital.

The factors behind this phenomenon are multiple: differences in capital accumulation, quality of infrastructures, technology, proximity to high-productive workers, different legal frameworks, etc. Wage differences among countries due to Place Premium are immense. The corollary is simple: more open borders would bring about a substantial reduction in poverty levels across the world.

In his paper 'Economics and Immigration: Trillion-Dollar Bills on the Sidewalk', Michael Clemens, senior fellow at the Center for Global Development, concludes that if all barriers to labour mobility were to be removed, world GDP would increase in the range of 50 per cent to 150 per cent. To use a more localised example: a worker from Guatemala or Nicaragua could triple her earnings simply by relocating to the US.

Even partial liberalisations would bring about considerable gains. For instance, a reform that allowed seven per cent of the population to emigrate to higher-productivity countries would result in an efficiency gain of ten per cent of world GDP.

To put this into perspective, if all remaining trade barriers were eliminated, world GDP would grow by just two to three per cent.

Surely the path to take is clear: immigration benefits everyone. Relaxing restrictions would mean more people could reap the benefits of capitalism – and the lives of millions of people across the globe would be improved.

26 June 2017

Poland scraps income tax for young people in bid to tempt emigrants home

The country has suffered from a 'brain drain' in recent years as young people go abroad for higher wages.

By Jon Stone, Europe Correspondent

Poland will this week scrap income tax for roughly two million young workers in a bid to tempt emigrants to return home.

1.7 million people have left Poland in the past 15 years, spurred on by higher wages and opportunities in western Europe.

Young people have disproportionately made use of the EU freedom of movement they have enjoyed since Poland joined the bloc in 2004 – and the government wants to reverse the trend.

'It's as if the entire city of Warsaw left, it's a gigantic loss,' Prime Minister Mateusz Morawiecki said.

'This must end, young people must stay in Poland.'

Mr Morawiecki added that opportunities for young people should 'match those available in the West'.

The widespread emigration has led to skills shortages, with every third employer in Poland reporting one.

Such skills shortages are highest in the construction, manufacturing, mining and transport sectors, according to a European Commission analysis.

From 1 August, Poles under the age of 26 who earn less than 85,528 zloty (£18,519) a year will not have to pay income tax. The threshold is high in comparison to the average salary in Poland, which is around 60,000 zloty a year.

Since 2016, the number of Polish people living abroad in other EU countries has been levelling off and more recently falling, according to the EU's statistics agency Eurostat.

The income tax cut is expected to help reverse a trend that has been happening naturally as incomes rise in Poland, partly thanks to economic integration with the EU, as well as substantial development aid.

The ruling right-wing populist Law and Justice (PiS) party proposed the policy ahead of the European Parliament elections earlier this year.

30 July 2019

Facts about refugees

Want the real facts about refugees? Here are the answers to some of the most common questions Refugee Action gets asked about asylum.

Q. What is a refugee?

A. According to the UN Refugee Convention, the definition of a refugee is someone who…

'Owing to a well-founded fear of being persecuted for reasons of race, religion, nationality, membership of a particular social group, or political opinion, is outside the country of his nationality, and is unable to or, owing to such fear, is unwilling to avail himself of the protection of that country' (Article 1, 1951 Convention Relating to the Status of Refugees).

Q. What is an asylum seeker?

A. The definition of an asylum seeker is someone who has arrived in a country and asked for asylum. Until they receive a decision as to whether or not they are a refugee, they are known as an asylum seeker. In the UK, this means they do not have the same rights as a refugee or a British citizen would. For example, asylum seekers aren't allowed to work.

The right to seek asylum is a legal right we all share. It isn't illegal to seek asylum, because seeking asylum is a legal process. It also isn't illegal to be refused asylum – it just means you haven't been able to meet the very strict criteria to prove your need for protection as a refugee.

Q. Are there many refugees and asylum seekers in the UK?

A. No. According to the United Nations High Commissioner for Refugees (UNHCR), by the end of 2018 there were 126,720 refugees, 45,244 pending asylum cases and 125 stateless persons in the UK. That's around one-quarter of a per cent (0.26%) of the UK's total population.

Q. Is the number of asylum seekers and refugees in the UK increasing?

A. Asylum applications to the UK are relatively low – 32,693 in the year to June 2019. This is significantly lower than the peak of 84,000 applications back in 2002.

Q. Which countries help the most refugees?

A. At the end of 2018, the country hosting the most refugees was Turkey – home to almost 3.7 million refugees. Other significant host countries for refugees were Pakistan (1.4 million), Uganda (1.2 million), Sudan (1.1 million), Iran (979,435) and Lebanon (949,666).

Q. How many Syrian refugees are there and how many is the UK helping?

A. According to the UNHCR, by the end of 2018 there were 6.7 million Syrian refugees worldwide. Around 4.6 million of these refugees are currently being hosted by just two countries – Turkey and Lebanon.

As well as providing aid to the refugee camps on Syria's borders, the UK has pledged to resettle 20,000 Syrians by 2020 through the Vulnerable Persons Resettlement Scheme. By June 2019, 17,051 Syrian refugees had come to the UK through this scheme.

Q. Which countries in Europe have the most asylum seekers?

A. In 2018, Germany received the highest number of asylum applications (161,900), and France the second most (114,500).

Q. Can asylum seekers work or claim benefits?

A. Asylum seekers are not allowed to claim benefits or work in the UK. If they are destitute and have no other means of supporting themselves, they can apply to receive asylum support. This is set at around £5.39 per day.

Q. What happens to someone when they get refugee status?

A. When a person is given refugee status, they have just 28 days to find accommodation and apply for mainstream benefits before they are evicted from asylum accommodation. Many refugees become homeless at this stage.

December 2016. Updated June 2019.

Refugees flee in record numbers around the world

The world's refugee population is growing. But the countries where migration is most contentious is not where most refugees are settling.

By Ben Barber

Conflict, poverty, violence and human rights violations are driving more people to flee their homelands than at any time since World War Two.

Last year, an estimated 13.6 million people were newly displaced due to conflict or persecution, raising the total number of individuals who have been forced to flee their homes to a record 70.8 million, according to a UN report.

The number of refugees 'is the highest number since we started tracking them,' said Sibylla Brodzinsky, a Washington spokeswoman for the UN High Commissioner for Refugees (UNHCR).

Of the displaced, 28 million – or 40% – fled to another country and are considered refugees, said Kathleen Newland, senior fellow at the Migration Policy Institute, a Washington think tank. Another 40 million fled from their homes but remained in their native country and are counted as 'internally displaced.'

Who are refugees?

According to the 1951 Convention on Refugees, a refugee is someone 'who is unable or unwilling to return to their country of origin owing to a well-founded fear of being persecuted for reasons of race, religion, nationality, membership of a particular social group, or political opinion.'

Two-thirds of refugees in 2018 came from just five countries, the UNHCR report noted: Syria (6.7 million), Afghanistan (2.7 million), South Sudan (2.3 million), Myanmar (1.1 million), Somalia (0.9 million). Venezuela is likely to move into the top five in 2019.

Although 85% of refugees come from poor and middle-income countries, it is conflict rather than poverty that drives migration, according to both Newland and Brodzinsky.

Some conflicts have deep and ancient roots – in race, language or religion – while others stem from fighting over scarce resources, such as farmland or water.

In the 1980s, refugees fled the Tamil Tiger insurgency in Sri Lanka. More recently some 700,000 ethnic Rohingya fled Myanmar to Bangladesh to escape ethnic persecution.

The causes of conflict often remain unresolved, forcing refugees to live in camps for years or even decades.

Some 350,000 Cambodians spent 13 years in camps in Thailand before finally returning to their homeland. The UN and other donors made their return possible by clearing landmines and rebuilding homes, roads and schools.

While many refugees return home, others end up resettling permanently elsewhere.

Benefits and backlashes

About three years ago, Germany and some other European countries opened their doors to resettle more than a million Syrians escaping civil war and ISIS Islamic terror.

Germany did not invite the refugees to settle merely for humanitarian reasons. The European nation knows it needs immigrants. As its population ages and its birth rate drops, it will increasingly depend on immigrants to work in factories and nursing homes.

But large refugee flows of the kind seen in the wake of the Syrian civil war can prompt popular backlashes.

Throughout much of Europe, the arrival of a million mainly young men from a different culture sparked an anti-immigrant backlash. Hungary and other Balkan nations threw up fences to bar refugees from entering their countries.

Ultimately, Europe, Turkey and Libya all agreed to introduce measures to stem the flow of refugees to wealthy nations. Their efforts were largely successful.

Turkey was paid billions of dollars to halt boats carrying refugees across a narrow strait to Greece. Other, sub-Saharan, refugees travelled to Libya and embarked on dangerous, flimsy boats towards Italy. Several European countries blocked them and tried to prevent humanitarian ships from encouraging refugee flows by coming to refugees' aid at sea.

Migrant arrivals to Italy dropped by 98 per cent in the first half of this year – to about 3,500 – from the 181,000 landed last year, the BBC reported 12 August. This drop followed the Government barring boats carrying refugees from landing at any Italian port.

Many of those who do reach European soil have faced long treks through snowy forests, in hopes of reaching Scandinavia, France or Britain. The Balkan states, Hungary, Czech Republic and Slovakia all refused to accept EU quotas of refugees. And Sweden, Germany and several other countries stopped accepting most asylum seekers, Newland said.

'Their efforts were largely successful – it did work,' she said. 'Europe was not stopped from taking some asylum claims, but the number accepted was greatly reduced after the March 2016 agreement with Turkey.'

Border politics

The United States has seen a surge in anti-immigrant sentiment, fanned in part by President Donald Trump, who has called Mexicans and other migrants rapists and criminals who threaten Americans' security.

In fact, UN and other officials say evidence shows migrants and refugees are less likely to commit crimes than native-born Americans. But accusations can become durable parts of modern mythology.

The Trump Administration has made blocking refugees and undocumented migrants one of its top priorities. It has tried to force refugees to seek asylum in the 'first safe country' they enter.

Host obligations

Despite intense coverage of refugees in Europe and the United States, most displaced persons seek refuge in countries that neighbour their homelands – perhaps with the hope of returning home later.

In 2018, the countries that hosted the most refugees were Turkey (3.7 million), Pakistan (1.4 million), Uganda (1.2 million), Sudan (1.1 million) and Germany (1.1 million).

With no end to conflict in sight and the world's population expected to increase in a few decades from eight billion today to ten billion, ever larger numbers of people will likely be on the move seeking safety and a better life.

That will likely put pressure on the UNHCR. The agency supplies food, water, medicine, schools and other basics to refugees. It also provides legal protection to prevent the exploitation of stateless people.

Rising numbers of migrants will also put pressure on the nearly 150 countries that have signed the 1951 Refugee Convention. That agreement bars signatories from sending refugees back to countries considered unsafe.

12 August 2019

More than 70 million people forced to flee their homes because of war and persecution

Sarah Newey, Global Health Security Correspondent

The number of people forced to flee their homes has hit an historic high, with more than 70 million people currently displaced by war, persecution and conflict, the UN's refugee agency has warned.

By the end of last year 70.8 million people were displaced globally – an increase of 2.3 million since 2017 and almost double the level of 20 years ago, the report found.

The figures – which include 41.3 million people displaced within their own country, 25.6 million refugees and 3.5 million asylum seekers (someone who has submitted an application for asylum in another country) – demonstrate that forced migration is 'becoming an entrenched norm', according to the UN's refugee agency, UNHCR.

'We have to come to terms with forced displacement as a result of war, because it is becoming an entrenched norm in the 21st century,' Adrian Edwards, spokesperson for the UNHCR, told *The Telegraph*. 'This reflects the very conflicted state of the world and 70.8 million people are paying the price.

'There is no indication of a significant reduction or plateau in these numbers – the trend suggests they will continue to rise,' he added.

The numbers, published in the agency's annual report, are the highest since the UNHCR began operations 70 years ago and include 13.6 million people who were forced to flee their homes last year, as well as some 56 million who have not been able to return to their communities for years.

In 2018, just 2.9 million people who had previously fled were able to go home.

Of those formally recognised as refugees, two-thirds come from just five countries – Syria, Afghanistan, South Sudan, Myanmar and Somalia.

But the numbers are likely to be an underestimate as the escalating economic and humanitarian crisis in Venezuela is only partially reflected.

While roughly 3.4 million people have fled the country, mostly travelling to other parts of Latin America and the

Caribbean, fewer than 500,000 have taken the step of formally applying for asylum.

Two-thirds of refugees came from just five countries

Number of refugees who fled home by the end of 2018 (millions)

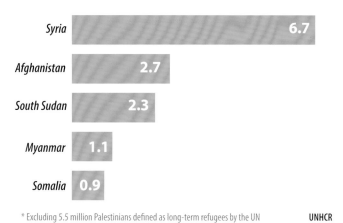

Syria	6.7
Afghanistan	2.7
South Sudan	2.3
Myanmar	1.1
Somalia	0.9

* Excluding 5.5 million Palestinians defined as long-term refugees by the UN   UNHCR

'What's happening with Venezuela is that many people are able to leave to neighbouring countries without needing visas or specific permits, so only around half a million are recognised formally as refugees or asylum seekers,' said Mr Edwards. 'But that number is growing and there are about 5,000 people leaving every day.

'It's the biggest displacement crisis anywhere in the world, second only to Syria.'

By the end of 2019, the UN predicts that at least five million people will have left the country. But the report warns that the mass exodus has already overwhelmed asylum procedures in neighbouring countries.

Mass internal movement in Ethiopia also drove an increase in global displacement in 2018, with violent clashes in the south and west forcing some 1.6 million people to flee their homes.

Syria saw the second–largest newly displaced population, with close to 900,000 people moving, while Nigeria saw more than 660,000 people forced from their homes last year.

Turkey welcomed the most refugees for the fifth consecutive year

Five countries which accepted the most refugees in 2018 (millions)

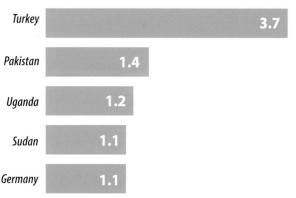

Turkey	3.7
Pakistan	1.4
Uganda	1.2
Sudan	1.1
Germany	1.1

UNHCR

Of those displaced, roughly half were children. Save the Children says the figures demonstrate a failure within the international community to tackle the root causes of conflict worldwide.

'We've seen a massive failing in states upholding the rules of war and as a result you just see many more children on the front line and a spike in the number of violations against children,' Keyan Salarkia, conflict and humanitarian policy adviser at Save the Children, told *The Telegraph*.

"Children should not be in a situation where they are forced to flee in the first place, but where they do flee they also need to be protected,' he added. 'The risk of sexual violence, trafficking and exploitation is high, certainly where they're unsupervised.'

This is the seventh year in a row that the number of refugees has hit an all-time high. But, according to the International Rescue Committee, the number of resettlement slots offered worldwide were cut by half between 2016 and 2017.

For the fifth consecutive year, Turkey hosted the largest number of refugees worldwide – some 3.7 million. Pakistan, Uganda, Sudan and Germany were the other major hosts of people seeking refuge.

The UN said that in 2018, 5,800 refugees resettled in the UK. This week, the Government announced it would welcome up to 6,000 more refugees between 2020 and 2021.

'Another year, another awful record broken,' said Ruth Tanner, head of humanitarian campaigns at Oxfam GB. "The [UK's] overseas aid to host countries and its new target to resettle 5,000 refugees per year are welcome and will go some way towards helping these people.

'But with 84 per cent of the world's refugees still in developing countries, wealthier nations should be doing more,' she added. 'One way the Government can do this is by making fairer rules on family reunion so that refugees can live with their loved ones in the UK.'

Alexander Carnwath, Unicef's senior policy advisor on migration and humanitarian crises, added: 'There is every risk that the number of displaced people will grow as the combined impact of conflict and climate change forces people from their homes.

'Therefore, Unicef calls on the international community to provide life-saving humanitarian aid, ensure communities have long-term access to essential services and put an end to grave violations against children.'

19 June 2019

Refugees in the UK

People sometimes use the terms 'refugee' and 'asylum seeker' interchangeably. But they're different.

The UK Government accepts someone as a refugee if he or she has fled their own country because of a 'well-founded fear of being persecuted for reasons of race, religion, nationality, membership of a particular social group or political opinion'.

Those words are from the Geneva Convention on refugees, a United Nations agreement that the UK is signed up to.

The Government also allows people to stay in the country to keep them safe without granting them refugee status as defined by the Geneva Convention. When we refer to 'refugees' or 'asylum grants' in this article, we're including these other forms of asylum, such as Humanitarian Protection or Leave Outside The Rules for human rights reasons.

An asylum seeker is someone who has applied to the Home Office for refugee status or one of those other forms of international protection, and is awaiting a decision on that application.

Asylum applications in the UK

In 2016, there were around 39,000 applications for asylum in the UK. That's including dependant family members of the main applicant. Those asylum seekers are counted among the estimated 600,000 immigrants to the UK in the 12 months to September 2016, most of whom come to work or study.

Many of those applications are rejected. Last year 21,000 people were turned down by the Home Office at the initial stage of the asylum process.

The annual success rate is more complicated than dividing 21,000 by 39,000, because of the time lag in making decisions, and because people can appeal the initial decision.

But we can say that over the past few years, excluding unknown outcomes, around half of asylum applications have ultimately been successful and the other half withdrawn or rejected.

UK asylum applications

Applications for refugee status or another form of international protection in the United Kingdom, including dependants

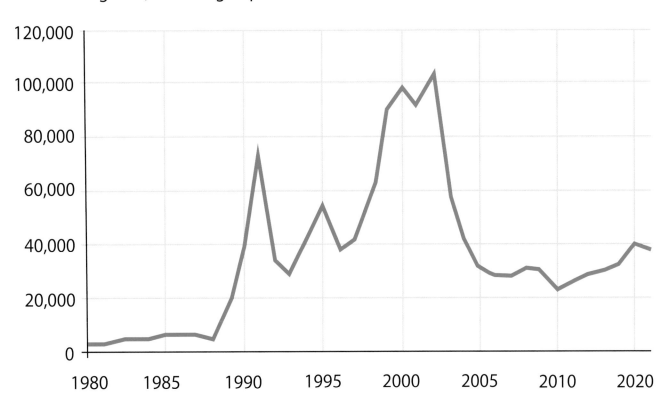

Source: Home Office, "Immigration Statistics, October to December 2016", asylum data tables, volume 1

Asylum application outcomes

Outcome analysis of asylum applications by year of application, as at May 2016

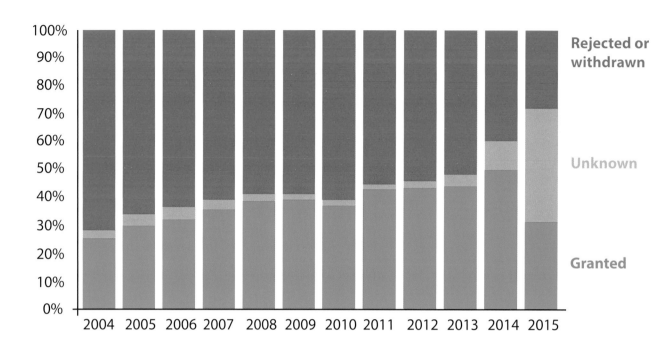

Source: Home Office, "Immigration Statistics, October to December 2016", asylum data tables

Refugees will generally get a residence permit for five years, and apply to settle in the UK permanently after that.

Asylum seekers and refugees in the UK

There were 33,000 asylum applications pending at the end of 2016, again including the dependants of applicants.

There may also be asylum seekers whose claim has been rejected that join the 'irregular migrant population', as immigration policy experts refer to it. Others might call them 'illegal immigrants'. It's hard to get a handle on how many failed asylum seekers are still here without permission, let alone the entire 'irregular' population.

There's no official figure for the number of refugees in the UK.

It partly depends on who you consider a 'refugee', given that people's residence status can change over time after being granted asylum. They may start on a time-limited residence permit, move to permanent residence, through to British citizenship.

Someone who arrived here in the country as a refugee – perhaps as a child – and is now a UK citizen might or might not still consider themselves a refugee.

The UN does publish annual estimates of the refugee population, which it's previously told us are based on the number of successful refugee applications in the previous 10 years – the assumption being that after a decade, a refugee will have become a citizen and no longer needs international protection.

On this fairly uncertain method, there were an estimated 123,000 refugees in the UK in 2015. That's around 0.2% of the population.

Where do refugees and asylum seekers come from?

Almost 90% of asylum seekers came from Asian or African countries in 2016. The top five nationalities for UK asylum applications were Iranian, Pakistani, Iraqi, Afghan and Bangladeshi.

In terms of asylum grants (before any appeal), Syrians topped the list, followed by Iranians, Eritreans, Sudanese and Afghans.

These figures don't include over 5,000 people resettled from other parts of the world, as distinct from coming to the UK to apply for asylum (you can't do so from another country). The vast majority of those have been Syrians.

6 March 2017

Locking people up is no answer to the global migrant crisis

By Phillipa Stroud

- ◆ Contrary to popular belief, most migration takes place between poor countries

- ◆ The proper answer to controlling migration is to help poor countries develop their economies

- ◆ While the media may focus on the Mexican border, the global migrant crisis is barely understood

Images of confused, caged children in foil blankets may have captured the media's attention this week, but they are symptomatic of a much bigger global refugee crisis that is still barely understood.

The footage from the Mexican border broke my heart as a mother and amazed me that these levels of inhumanity were possible in the 21st century. It was deeply uncomfortable. But at least the cameras were there to record the monstrous injustice.

I am even more concerned about the places where the suffering goes untroubled by TV cameras. Specifically, I am worried about the staggering 66 million people who have been forcibly displaced globally – equivalent to uprooting the entire UK population.

At Legatum, we believe this global refugee crisis is the humanitarian issue of our time. And things are getting worse, with the highest levels of displacement on record this year. This crisis requires an urgent response from governments to work together to address the causes of fragile states and do their fair share for displaced people.

Instead, the headlines on World Refugee Day this year were about President Trump's aggressive, populist campaign on the Mexican border, where families have been forcibly separated. Governments are baffled, with no coherent policy response.

Global people movement is not the one-dimensional story many imagine. We think we know about young, able migrants from poor countries seeking prosperity in rich countries, swelling 'jungle camps' on borders like Calais or Lampedusa island. No, the real crisis is playing out unseen in places where many fear to visit. It is where 'irregular' journeys take place to the lowest income countries such as Ethiopia, driven by displacement, war and desperation.

In the Legatum Institute's new report, *Global People Movements*, we find that governments around the world lack the data to properly assess the scale and severity of the challenge, preventing them from formulating an effective policy response. We have a tragedy unfolding, and few effective solutions.

Contrary to conventional images of economic migrants gravitating to rich host countries for a new life of wealth-creation, most migrant journeys are to neighbouring countries in the low-to-middle income bracket within their region of origin. The lowest income countries, least capable of resourcing the burden, host as much as 30% of the global total of refugees. Conditions are often miserable.

Registered refugees represent a tiny fraction of all the migrants who are vulnerable or driven by necessity. The number of individuals forcibly displaced (internally and cross-border) has reached a record high. Of the 66 million people experiencing forced displacement, approximately 40 million are internally displaced in countries such as Nigeria and Syria.

While conflict is a well-recognised cause of migration, it is high levels of socio-economic vulnerability, a climate of insecurity and natural hazards that also drive people movement. Migrants are frequently exposed to intolerable levels of risk in transit. Irregular migrants who often lack paperwork and therefore official protection face dangerous journeys.

They are unprotected, they accumulate and become trapped by debt with no legal recourse. The limited opportunities for legal migration forces individuals to use people smugglers, where there is a risk of being trafficked. Migrants who fall prey to human traffickers can be exploited in both transit and destination countries.

The number of identified victims of human trafficking could represent less than 1% of the true number. During the migrant journey, the fine line with human trafficking – the acquisition of people by force, fraud or deception with the aim of exploiting them – can be easily crossed. This is one of the primary causes of modern slavery.

22 June 2018

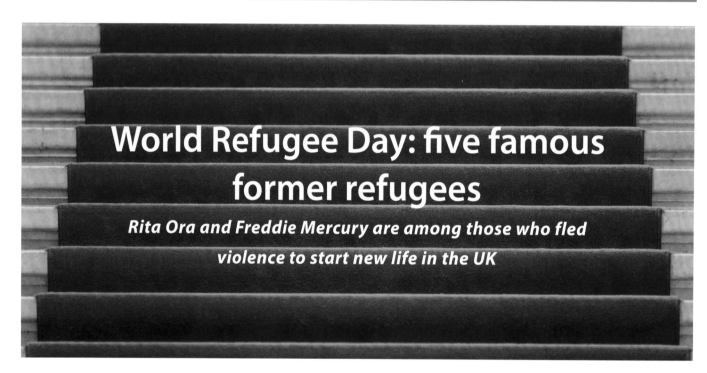

World Refugee Day: five famous former refugees

Rita Ora and Freddie Mercury are among those who fled violence to start new life in the UK

World Refugee Day is when the UN recognises the struggles and triumphs of displaced people around the world who have been forced from their homes by violence, prejudice or persecution.

To mark the day, here are five famous figures who started life as refugees:

Freddie Mercury

The legendary Queen frontman was born Farrokh Bulsara to Indian parents living in the British protectorate of Zanzibar, now part of Tanzania.

In 1964, the family left to escape the violence of the Zanzibar Revolution, in which the local African population rose up against the island's Arab and Indian minorities.

Mercury, then aged 17, and his family started a new life in Middlesex. Six years later, he would meet guitarist Brian May and drummer Roger Taylor – and the rest is history.

Mila Kunis

Hollywood star Kunis was born in Ukraine in 1983, when the country was part of the Soviet Union.

Her parents, aware of the limited political and economic freedom in the communist state, sought refuge in the US in 1991, when the future star was seven years old.

Kunis has spoken in the past about the trauma of her first year of school in New York, unable to speak English. She remains a fluent Russian speaker, and frequently gives interviews in her native tongue.

Andrew Sachs

The actor, best known for his portrayal of hapless Spanish waiter Manuel in *Fawlty Towers*, was born in Berlin as Andreas Sachs, the child of a Jewish father and Catholic mother. The family fled Germany in 1938 to escape the growing danger of Nazi persecution, and settled in north London.

Popular legend has it that when *Fawlty Towers* was sold for broadcast in Germany, Sachs reprised his role as Manuel for the German dub - complete with Spanish accent.

Rita Ora

Ora and her family escaped war-torn Kosovo in 1991, when the singer was a year old.

In 2013, Ora recalled how she, her sister and their parents had lived in a single room when they first arrived in London as penniless refugees. However, she told the *London Evening Standard* that her childhood hardships had made her stronger.

'That word [refugee] carries a lot of prejudice,' she said. 'But it also made us determined to survive.'

Henry Kissinger

Former US Secretary of State Henry Kissinger was born into a German Jewish family, who escaped the Nazi regime in 1938, arriving in New York via London when he was 15 years old.

Kissinger served in the US Army's Counter Intelligence Corps during the Second World War, before going into politics.

A foreign policy expert, he became President Nixon's security adviser and received the 1973 Nobel Peace Prize for his role in negotiating an end to the Vietnam war.

Kissinger is not the only former refugee to serve as Secretary of State. Madeleine Albright, the first woman appointed to the office, was granted asylum in the US aged 11 after her family fled communist persecution in their native Czechoslovakia.

20 June 2018

Key Facts

- There were an estimated 144.7 million passenger arrivals in the year ending June 2019 (including returning UK residents), a 4% increase compared to the previous year and the highest number on record. (page 1)

- There were 185,465 work-related visas granted in the year ending June 2019, 11% higher than the previous year, and the highest level since the year ending March 2009. (page 1)

- There were 169,606 visas granted for family reasons in the year ending June 2019, 20% more than in the previous year. (page 1)

- The UK gave protection to 18,519 people in the year ending June 2019 (up 29% compared with the previous year). (page 2)

- According to the United Nations, the United States has the highest number of immigrants (foreign-born individuals), with 48 million in 2015. (page 3)

- The smaller the country, the higher its probable proportion of foreign-born residents. (page 4)

- According to the United Nations, there were 258 million immigrants in 2017, representing only a small minority of the world population (3.4%); the vast majority of people live in their country of birth. (page 5)

- Since the EU referendum in late June 2016, the estimated number of EU nationals immigrating to the UK fell from 284,000 the year before the vote to 226,000 in the year after. That's now down to 202,000. (page 6)

- Around 3.7 million people living in the UK in 2018 were citizens of another EU country. That's about 6% of the UK population. (page 7)

- 1.3 million people born in the UK live in other EU countries, according to 2017 estimates from the United Nations (UN). (page 8)

- Spain hosts the largest group of UK citizens: an estimated 310,000 UK-born people lived there in 2017. Ireland is second with 280,000 and France third with 190,000. (page 9)

- A recent Gallup World Poll poll reveals that 15% of the global population – over 750 million people – would migrate if they could. (page 11)

- One in five migrants chose the US as their favoured destination in 2017. (page 12)

- In all countries except France, the most commonly agreed benefit of immigration has been better food. (page 15)

- The most commonly given downside of immigration is increased crime. It is especially likely to be cited in Denmark, Sweden, Germany and Norway (at between 62% and 68%). (page 16)

- An estimated 500,000 EU citizens are working in low-skilled jobs in the UK such as picking fruit, cleaning offices, working in warehouses and food factories. (page 19)

- According to the United Nations High Commissioner for Refugees (UNHCR), by the end of 2018 there were 126,720 refugees, 45,244 pending asylum cases and 125 stateless persons in the UK. That's around one-quarter of a per cent (0.26%) of the UK's total population. (page 30)

- Asylum applications to the UK are relatively low – 32,693 in the year to June 2019. This is significantly lower than the peak of 84,000 applications back in 2002. (page 30)

- At the end of 2018, the country hosting the most refugees was Turkey – home to almost 3.7 million refugees. Other significant host countries for refugees were Pakistan (1.4 million), Uganda (1.2 million), Sudan (1.1 million), Iran (979,435) and Lebanon (949,666). (page 31)

- According to the UNHCR, by the end of 2018 there were 6.7 million Syrian refugees worldwide. Around 4.6 million of these refugees are currently being hosted by just two countries – Turkey and Lebanon. (page 31)

- The UK has pledged to resettle 20,000 Syrians by 2020 through the Vulnerable Persons Resettlement Scheme. By June 2019, 17,051 Syrian refugees had come to the UK through this scheme. (page 31)

- Asylum seekers are not allowed to claim benefits or work in the UK. If they are destitute and have no other means of supporting themselves, they can apply to receive asylum support. This is set at around £5.39 per day. (page 31)

- By the end of 2018 70.8 million people were displaced globally – an increase of 2.3 million since 2017 and almost double the level of 20 years ago, the report found. (page 33)

Assimilation

Assimilation is the process by which immigrants gradually adapt and blend in to the way of life of their host country.

Asylum application

If a person wishes to stay in the UK as a refugee, they must apply for asylum. To be eligible they must have left their country and be unable to go back because they fear persecution. Refugees should apply for asylum as soon as they arrive in the UK.

Asylum seeker

The refugee council defines an asylum seeker as 'a person who has left their country of origin and formally applied for asylum in another country but whose application has not yet been concluded'.

Detention centre

A centre used for the short-term detention of illegal immigrants and refugees.

Economic migrant

Someone who has chosen to move to another country in order to work. Refugees are not economic migrants.

Emigrant

A person who leaves their own country in order to settle in another.

Expat

A person who lives outside their native country.

Immigrant

Someone who comes to live in a country from another country in order to take up residence.

Internally displaced person

Someone who has fled their home but remains within their own country.

International Humanitarian Law (IHL)

A set of rules and principles that govern armed conflict. IHL protects refugees from States that are involved in armed conflict.

Jungle camp

The nickname given to refugee camps, like the camp set up near Calais, France, inhabited by migrants and refugees trying to reach the UK.

Migrant

A person who is moving or has moved across an international border or within a State away from his/her habitual place of residence.

Overstayer

A person who was permitted to stay in the UK for a limited period of time and who has remained longer than this time.

Refugee

A person who has left their home country and cannot return because they fear that they will be persecuted on the grounds of race, religion, nationality, political affiliation or social group. In the UK, a person is officially known as a refugee when they claim asylum and this claim is accepted by the Government.

Refugee camp

A camp that provides shelter/temporary housing for refugees or displaced persons. The world's largest refugee camp is Dadaab in Kenya. The camp hosts 35,000 people in five camps.

Residence permit

An official document allowing a person to legally reside in a country they were not born in.

Statelessness

Statelessness refers to a lack of nationality, which can occur because of the redrawing of borders, or holes in nationality laws.

United Nations High Commissioner for Refugees (UNHCR)

The Office of the United Nations High Commissioner for Refugees was established in 1950 and aims to 'lead and coordinate international action to protect refugees and resolve refugee problems worldwide'.

Visa

Official permission to enter a country for a temporary stay within a specified time period.

Windrush

The *Empire Windrush* was a British troopship carrying hundreds of passengers from the Caribbean hoping for a new life in Britain. There was a significant labour shortage in post-war UK and most of the Windrush passengers were attracted by the job opportunities. The ship arrived in Tilbury Docks, Essex on 21 June 1948.

Activities

Brainstorming

- In small groups, discuss what you know about migration and immigration. Consider the following:

  - What is the definition of migration?

  - What is the definition of immigration?

  - What's the difference between a refugee and an immigrant?

  - Are the terms, 'refugee' and 'migrant' used correctly in the articles you have seen?

  - Why might people choose to migrate?

- In pairs, write a pro and con list of things that might affect a person's decision to move to a new country.

Research

- Research the asylum process in the UK and, in small groups, discuss your findings and whether you believe the process is fair.

- Research the movement of refugees after the Second World War and write some notes that explore your findings. Share your notes with the rest of your class.

- Choose a country in Europe and research how many migrants there are in that country. Are they EU or non-EU migrants? Write a short report.

- Do some research on the history of immigration. Create a timeline showing periods of mass immigration. Use the www.ourmigrationstory.org.uk website to help you.

- In small groups, create a questionnaire to find out opinions of immigration. Consider the difference between EU and non-EU migrants.

- Do some research on the area that you live, are there many migrants there? If so, where are they from?

Design

- Choose one of the articles in this topic and create an illustration to highlight the key themes/messages of your chosen article.

- Design a leaflet explaining what a person from another part of the world might expect when they arrive in Britain.

Oral

- As a class, discuss the statement 'We should all be free to live where we choose.'

- Choose one of the illustrations from this topic and, in pairs, discuss why the artist decided to depict the themes they did.

- Conduct a survey in class asking people 'If you had to migrate to another country, where would you go and why?'

- In small groups, discuss why you think so many migrants/refugees are willing to risk their lives in order to reach Europe.

Reading/writing

- 'What are the main reasons people become refugees? What other reasons drive people from their homes?' Answer on no more than one side of A4.

- Write a diary entry from the point of view of a young person living in either:

  - a detention centre in the UK.

  - a US-Mexico border detention camp.

- Choose two newspapers, and, over the course of a week, cut out all the articles that talk about refugees/migrants. At the end of the week write one-paragraph answers to the following questions:

  - Are the terms, 'refugee' and 'migrant' used correctly in the articles you have seen?

  - Is press coverage largely positive or negative?

  - What are the key issues identified?

- Imagine you have moved to the UK from another country in search of work. Write about some of the issues you may face.

- Write a persuasive letter to the prime minister arguing why it is a good thing to allow people to migrate to the UK to work.

- Write a postcard from an immigrant to a friend in their home country. Are they enjoying living and working in a new country?

Acknowledgements

The publisher is grateful for permission to reproduce the material in this book. While every care has been taken to trace and acknowledge copyright, the publisher tenders its apology for any accidental infringement or where copyright has proved untraceable. The publisher would be pleased to come to a suitable arrangement in any such case with the rightful owner.

Images

Cover image courtesy of iStock. All other images courtesy of Pixabay, rawpixel.com and Unsplash.

Illustrations

Don Hatcher: pages 12 & 37 Simon Kneebone: pages 2 & 27 Angelo Madrid: pages 25 & 32.

Additional acknowledgements

With thanks to the Independence team: Shelley Baldry, Danielle Lobban, Jackie Staines and Jan Sunderland.

Tracy Biram

Cambridge, September 2019